BOOK AWARDS FOR *RAISING TECH-HEALTHY HUMANS*

2023

WINNER: BEST INDIE BOOK AWARD - BEST NON-FICTION PARENTING BOOK (USA)

WINNER: eLIT AWARDS - BEST PARENTING EBOOK (USA)

SILVER: IBPA BENJAMIN FRANKLIN AWARD - BEST NON-FICTION AUDIOBOOK (USA)

SHORTLISTED: AUSTRALIAN CHRISTIAN BOOK OF THE YEAR (AUSTRALIA)

PRAISE FOR *RAISING TECH-HEALTHY HUMANS*

'What a relief and a joy to find a book on parenting that is so well set out, so clear, so easy and fun to read. Daniel Sih writes with such personality and humility you feel that you know him, and he is on the journey with you. Every household is grappling with this stuff – but suddenly reading Daniel's book, it not only feels manageable, but really proactive and – surprisingly – heroic to take back our true job as parents – makers of fantastic human beings. This book somehow manages to be so simple, and yet so satisfyingly deep. This book is about freedom, and love, and choice. Well done, Daniel Sih.'
— **STEVE BIDDULPH**, BEST-SELLING AUTHOR OF *MANHOOD*, *RAISING BOYS* AND *RAISING GIRLS*

'*Raising Tech-Healthy Humans* is a readable, practical guide for parents who want to help their kids achieve screen life–real life balance.'
— **DAVID MURROW**, BEST-SELLING AUTHOR OF *DROWNING IN SCREEN TIME*

'A great reminder that going with the tech flow is not always the best way to love and support our kids. This book has inspired me to make different choices as a mum.'
— **BELINDA**, PARENT OF 7 AND 9 YEAR OLDS

'A practical and encouraging book to help parents face the difficult dilemmas of how to set wise boundaries around technology in their homes.'
— **DR AMY IMMS**, AUTHOR, FOUNDER OF THE BURNOUT PROJECT

'*Raising Tech Healthy Humans* could not arrive at a better time for parents who are desperate for help. It stands as a guard rail against Big Tech's erosion of the safety and wellbeing of our young. This accessible, easy-to-read guidebook will assist parents in the weighty responsibility of raising good humans bearing essential qualities of patience, emotional regulation, empathy, goodness and self-awareness. A vital resource for every caring parent.'
— **MELINDA TANKARD REIST**, AUTHOR, SPEAKER, AND MOVEMENT DIRECTOR OF COLLECTIVE SHOUT

'Are you a parent or caregiver feeling overwhelmed by raising children in the digital world? In less than ninety minutes, you will find the support, guidance, and relief you're looking for.'
— **CHRIS McKENNA**, FOUNDER OF PROTECT YOUNG EYES

'I love the vulnerability and honesty of this book as Daniel navigates what parenting looks like in a tech-savvy world. There's no judgement of the mistakes we make, but practical, simple ideas to guide us.'
— **MICHELLE DEMPSEY**, CHIEF EXECUTIVE OFFICER, CHRISTIAN EDUCATION NATIONAL

'I got a phone later than most of my friends but when I finally got it I felt like I actually didn't need it. Now, I only use it when it's helpful and I'm glad I waited until I was older.'
— **NAOMI**, 15 YEARS OLD (DANIEL'S DAUGHTER)

'A timely and incredibly important contribution to the world. This book is an instant lifesaver to parents battling for the future of their children's hearts and minds.'
— **JAEMIN FRAZER**, AUTHOR, TEDx SPEAKER, AND FOUNDER OF THE INSECURITY PROJECT

'A wonderful parenting handbook to teach adults to be good role models and help children connect with real people and enjoy their life without being dependent on devices.'
— **RICHARD STOKES**, CHIEF EXECUTIVE OFFICER, AUSTRALIAN BOARDING SCHOOLS ASSOCIATION

'This easy little book is packed with straightforward research, advice and encouragement. Parents are going to love it!'
— **SUSY LEE**, AWARD-WINNING AUTHOR OF *RAISING KIDS WHO CARE*

'Daniel's book is a treasure trove of simple and practical tips for families to develop strategies to set up their children with healthier tech routines and screen-based habits. Read it, digest it, and use it!'
— **DR MARK DUNWOODY**, AUTHOR, CO-FOUNDER OF HEALTHY RHYTHMS INSTITUTE

'Daniel Sih has written a concise, practical and very readable guide that parents of school-age children will not only relate to but learn from.'
— **EAMONN POLLARD**, PRINCIPAL, ST ALOYSIUS CATHOLIC COLLEGE

'This book has helped us so much in our parenting journey. It reinforced our values to hold off on a phone a little longer, and has enabled helpful conversations with our kids.'
— **LEANNE AND MATT**, PARENTS OF 8 AND 12 YEAR OLDS

'A powerful parenting model of walking side by side with our kids as they navigate the digital world. We loved Daniel's vulnerable approach, sharing his own parental wins and failures in a way that captured our emotions and made us laugh out loud.'
— **KATIE AND DAVE KOBLER**, DIRECTORS OF YOUR CHOICEZ

CHRISTIAN PARENTING SPECIAL EDITION

RAISING TECH-HEALTHY HUMANS

HOW TO RESET YOUR CHILDREN'S TECH HABITS AND GIVE THEM A GREAT START TO LIFE

DANIEL SIH

First published in 2023 by Daniel Sih

© Daniel Sih 2023
The moral rights of the author have been asserted

All rights reserved. Except as permitted under the *Australian Copyright Act 1968* (for example, a fair dealing for the purposes of study, research, criticism or review), no part of this book may be reproduced, stored in a retrieval system, communicated or transmitted in any form or by any means without prior written permission.

All inquiries should be made to the author.

Book production and text design by Publish Central
Cover design by Pipeline Design

Disclaimer: The material in this publication is of the nature of general comment only, and does not represent professional advice. It is not intended to provide specific guidance for particular circumstances and it should not be relied on as the basis for any decision to take action or not take action on any matter which it covers. Readers should obtain professional advice where appropriate, before making any such decision. To the maximum extent permitted by law, the author and publisher disclaim all responsibility and liability to any person, arising directly or indirectly from any person taking or not taking action based on the information in this publication.

To my friend, Michael Verdouw, who taught me so much about loving life and raising humans before leaving this earth far too quickly.

To my mum, Wendy Fuller, who has modelled consistency and unconditional love.

And to my wife, Kylie Sih, who is a constant source of joy, wisdom and inspiration to so many. Thank you for helping us all become better humans.

I don't want to get to the end of my life and find that I just lived the length of it. I want to live the width of it as well.
  POET AND NATURALIST DIANE ACKERMAN

FREE ONLINE VIDEO SERIES

Struggling to raise kids in a screen-filled world?

I've created an online tech-parenting course to help you expand on the ideas in this book.

This free tech-parenting course includes:

- 15 high-quality videos
- Print-ready infographics
- Downloadable checklists
- Digital contracts... and more!

Sign up to receive this exclusive pack of bonus resources.

Visit www.raisinghumans.au/faith or scan the QR Code to get started.

    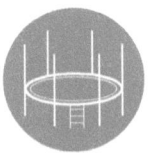

CONTENTS

Preface	xii
Who should read this book?	xv
Introduction: The real-world struggle	xix
PART I: SETTING THE SCENE	**1**
1. Raise adults, not children	5
2. A healthy brain first	9
3. Life-giving limits	21
PART II: THE STARTER FRAMEWORK	**29**
4. Start with self	35
5. Take it slowly	45
6. Age-appropriate setup	57
7. Regular talk	71
8. Tech-healthy rhythms	79
9. Encourage adventures	87
10. Rely on others	97
PART III: THE PATH FORWARD	**105**
11. The STARTER Framework checklist	109
Conclusion	113
Appendix: 100 fun non-screen activities to do with children	117
Free parenting resources	121
Acknowledgements	125
Notes	131
Index	139
About the author	141

PREFACE

I remember attending a church service where an elderly man gave a communion talk. He had attended church for forty years and, by his calculation, had received the sacrament of Communion more than two thousand times. 'Communion is a powerful ritual,' he explained from the pulpit. 'Think about how significant this ritual has been in forming my head, heart and habits.' It was a good point. Two thousand wafers of bread. Two thousand sips of communion wine. Over a lifetime, this ritual must have deeply impacted his world view.

At the same time, while this gentleman was talking, I couldn't help but notice a young boy next to me, swiping his iPad. He was about seven years old and engrossed in a game of Angry Birds. Rather than paying attention to the speaker, the boy was annihilating an army of grunting green pigs.

I admit I found this somewhat distracting. I should have been focusing on the Lord's Supper, but instead I was mesmerised by the boy and his game. It felt like two worlds colliding; an old and young man shaped by old and new habits. The former had taken forty years to experience communion two thousand times. But it would take just a few days for the latter to swipe his screen two thousand times.

As we ate and drank communion that morning, a thought crossed my mind, 'If a shared table can transform one's head, heart and habits in such a powerful way, I wonder what the impact of swiping a screen might be on a child's spiritual formation? I wonder how the devices we give our children might form their heart, head and habits?'

DIGITAL TECHNOLOGY AND DISCIPLESHIP

Research has discovered a profound connection between what we do on a regular basis and who we become. The habits we form online will inevitably shape our character and our beliefs. According to Orthodox author Rod Dreher, 'Technology is a kind of liturgy that teaches us to frame our experiences in the world in certain ways and that, if we aren't careful, profoundly distorts our relationship to God, to other people, and to the material world — and even our self-understanding.' In other words, if we reach for our phone first thing in the morning and last thing at night, saturating our lives with constant connectivity, we may find our beliefs and world views shifting in line with the goals of Silicon Valley tech companies rather than the teachings of Jesus. This is true for both adults and children.

The role of the Church has always been to form people in the ways of Jesus by capturing their hearts, renewing their minds, and shaping their habits. Technology can be wonderful and incredibly important when used as a tool, in age-appropriate ways, but it makes a lousy god when used too often, without due care. It is important, therefore, that we learn to approach technology in a wise and intentional way to give our kids a fantastic start to life, both online and offline. Our use of technology is a discipleship issue because it's about how our children are being formed, towards or away from faith. If our children are to love God with all of their heart, mind, soul and strength, the way they use their time and focus their attention is critically important.

This is why I wrote the Christian Schools Edition of *Raising Tech-Healthy Humans*, to support parents who want their kids to grow up with Christian values and godly behaviours, helped rather than hindered by the technologies they use. As a dedicated Christ-follower with more than a decade of experience as a church pastor, I have come to the conclusion that establishing tech-healthy habits is one of the most important things we can do for our children's faith development (as well as our own).

This special edition is written for school communities, rather than individuals, to make it easier for everyone to raise tech-healthy humans. Parenting children is hard work – let alone parenting in a world surrounded by technological change! It is incredibly hard to swim against the tide of digital overuse as an individual. But if we rally together as school communities – teachers and parents supporting healthier tech-choices for our kids – then it becomes easier for everyone. It is easier to create healthy tech and non-tech patterns at home, when others are doing the same. It is easier to delay giving social media to your children when the majority of parents are saying 'not yet' as well. My aim isn't for everyone to think or act in the same way, for every child is different and every family unique, but if we can share ideas and talk about technology together, then we will be more equipped to support each other in the wonderfully complex task of raising tech-healthy humans.

Ultimately, this book is not about saying 'no' to screens. It's not about screen-time limits, or cyber safety, or internet filtering, even though I cover these ideas in practical ways. Instead, this is a book about the life we want for our children – no matter what your faith tradition may be. It's about discovering a greater 'yes' that involves riding bikes, climbing trees, praying as families, reading books, singing songs, baking cakes, making sandcastles, playing board games, eating with friends, and myriad activities that make childhood rich and exciting beyond the glowing rectangle. Let's enjoy the best of the online world but not be diminished by too much technology, and raise a generation of healthy, faith-filled kids who love God and love others in beautiful, life-giving ways.

WHO SHOULD READ THIS BOOK?

As parents, we are stretched for time. It's hard enough to get our children to their next soccer game, let alone carve out time to read a long book.

That's why I have written a practical parenting handbook for people like myself who are run off their feet and in need of solutions. It contains essential information to help parents make informed tech choices for their children, without the faff.

And while I wrote this book to be read in about two hours, I want to ensure that your time is well spent. Space is precious. So, before you dive in, please take a few minutes to read the next few pages to discover if this book is a smart investment of your focus and energy.

As a productivity trainer, professional speaker and award-winning author, I speak at conferences around Australia about the impact of digital overuse on our health, happiness and productivity. Typically these events are for leaders, managers and professionals who are always online and in need of more space.

And whenever I speak, someone invariably asks me a parenting question: 'Can you help my child make space and unplug from their screens?'

So, I wrote this book.

Raising Tech-Healthy Humans is a guidebook specifically for parents with primary school–aged children (between 5 and 12 years old), who are concerned about the impacts of digital overuse on their child's development.* These parents are insightful enough to realise that 'doing what everyone else is doing' is a recipe for hardship. They are brave enough to take action for the health of their children, even when this is hard. They are positive enough to seek solutions.

As I speak with parents across the country, there is a growing awareness and concern about the adverse effects of screens on our children's health and happiness. Some of us have extensive knowledge about this. Others simply have an intuitive sense that something is amiss. Almost all of us are observant enough to see that too much time on a device has negative side effects on our children's behaviour.

You may be concerned about the growing epidemic of anxiety among young people and the impact of social media on their mental health. You may be aware of the growing evidence of a connection between excessive online gaming and ADHD. You may be worried about the darker side of the web, such as online grooming or pornography. Or you may simply be frustrated by how hard it is to get your child off their iPad, and long

---

* Throughout this book, I will use the generic terms 'children' or 'kids' to refer to primary school–aged children, who in Australia are 5 to 12 years old. 'Pre-school children' are younger than this, and 'teenagers' are older. The term 'pre-teens' or 'tweens' will be used to describe 9- to 12-year-old children who are at or near the end of primary school and soon to enter high school.

for the days when kids rode bikes, climbed trees and played board games with their friends.

Whatever your reasons for picking up this book, my aim is to help you establish better tech habits and routines with your children and pre-teens. Rather than write a long, detailed book about *why* we need to change, my aim is to focus on practical advice about *how* to make a start. My assumption is you have a base-level of knowledge about why too much time online or looking at a screen is concerning. For the purposes of this book, it's enough to realise that children become irritable and emotionally labile when they spend all day swiping on a device.

For those who like a bit more detail, I have outlined three essential ideas about why change is needed in Part I: Setting the scene. There are also links at the back of the book with recommended reading and resources. We then move to practical applications in Part II: The STARTER Framework, and finish with a checklist of next actions in Part III: The path forward. If you are a concerned parent and ready to implement positive change immediately, this is the book for you.

To be clear, *Raising Tech-Healthy Humans* is *not* primarily for:

- parents who see no problems with digital technology or with their children spending large amounts of time on a screen
- parents whose children struggle with significant mental health problems like severe anxiety, depression, self-harm or addiction, and require professional help
- parents whose teenagers are already addicted to their phones and are out of control (tech advice for teens is different than for children and pre-teens)
- educators who are seeking to understand how to implement better tech policies in their schools

- theory-focused parents who want a deep dive into the research behind digital addiction and overuse
- hermits who live in the wilderness and have not yet heard of the internet!

This book *is* perfect for parents who want:

- to develop practical strategies to set up their children with healthier tech routines and screen-based habits
- practical advice about when and how to get their children their own devices; in particular, their first phone
- guidance on how to establish healthier boundaries and limits on their children's online habits
- thought-provoking frameworks to develop positive non-digital routines and digital-free spaces as a family
- practical encouragement to help take the next steps.

My passion is to help you and your children make space to think and live differently. *Raising Tech-Healthy Humans* does not contain everything you could know about tech-healthy parenting. It is overwhelming being a parent and surviving is hard enough. This is why I have done my best to write a concise, practical and helpful book. This is the Spacemakers approach – to reduce and eliminate clutter, to give you space. I hope there is enough information to help you take the next steps without overwhelming you with excess noise.

If this sounds worthwhile to you, please keep reading.

INTRODUCTION

THE REAL-WORLD STRUGGLE

It was a Saturday. A family day. A time to connect and enjoy time together. Better still, it was the first day of the school holidays and a day with no plans. We had no soccer games to drive to or birthday parties to attend. Just a brand-new day to be together and make memories.

But rather than starting the day with connection and joy, my kids and I descended into an argument.

I had been stuck in my office all week and was keen for a family outing. I came upstairs with a spring in my step, entered the lounge room and chirpily exclaimed, 'Good morning!' My two sons, 10 and 12 years old, ignored me, and this annoyed me. My boys were vegging out on the couch, still in their pyjamas, streaming their favourite shows on separate laptops. They were engrossed in their online activities.

It was like I didn't exist.

So I repeated my 'good morning', but replaced my chirpy Saturday-morning-happy-voice with a grumpy-daddy-bear-tone. It got a response. Kind of. Without looking up from their screens, my tweens grunted something in unison that sounded more like 'gomong' than 'good morning, dear father'.

This pushed my buttons, big time.

'Okay, boys, close your laptops.' My voice was louder than necessary. 'How long have you been online?'

Now on the defensive, my boys told me it had only been two hours (which is technically fine as they are allowed 2.5 hours on a Saturday). But rather than check my own emotions and de-escalate the situation, I became an inquisitor: 'Why are you still in your pyjamas?' 'Have you eaten your breakfast?' 'Why haven't you eaten your breakfast … you know the rules, no screens before breakfast.' Backed into a corner, the boys pushed back, arguing that it wasn't fair because they weren't doing anything wrong: 'We've only been watching two hours and this is our holidays!' 'We don't need breakfast because we're not babies.' 'Why are you so grumpy?' And so on and so forth.

So, rather than a positive, life-giving start to the day, we ended up in a meaningless argument. I snapped. They sulked. My wife became angry because I had raised my voice at the children. My 15-year-old daughter – who had been dozing in bed – wisely stayed in her room for the next few hours rather than entering a warzone.

A fun day in the Sih household!

Upon reflection, I could have approached this interaction differently. Yes, I was frustrated that my children didn't 'good morning' me, but this was a pretence to offload other resentments. I found it hard to see my kids glued to their laptops first thing in the morning. I was harbouring resentment that they had refused to go swimming the weekend before, choosing to mooch around the house instead. I was frustrated by how much time I had spent on my own laptop that week, working nights to smash out a deadline rather than being with my family. All of these annoyances created a melting pot where I exploded, turning a potentially positive Saturday into a storm of negativity and rule setting.

I start with this parenting stuff-up with hesitation, for my children are amazing and I'm not always a tyrant. While it can be a battle to inspire my children to embrace life outdoors, they are not addicted to their screens. But I also struggle, like we all do, to raise children in our always-on culture. I live and parent in the real world, struggling with real mistakes and real anxieties.

So, rather than a list of credentials, my primary qualification for writing this book is that I am an engaged, imperfect parent trying my best. Like you, I make my fair share of mistakes. Like you, I raise my voice when I should be patient. Like you, I feel parent guilt and parent frustrations. I win some days and lose some weeks. While I want to give my children more attention, some days I feel so mentally and physically exhausted that all I can do is lie on the couch and swipe my phone (while telling my children not to do the same). All of this is to say that I'm stumbling along, just like you, parenting on the run and hoping my children will turn out better than I deserve.

This book is written for imperfect parents like you and me. That is, real people with real battles and real blunders. I do not have a perfect family and don't profess to have a perfect set of parenting techniques. But I have learnt a thing or two during my time as a parent, backed by years of experience as a productivity consultant who is deeply immersed in the technology space. I hope the strategies in this book will fast forward the learning process for you as you seek to raise tech-healthy humans.

PART I
SETTING THE SCENE

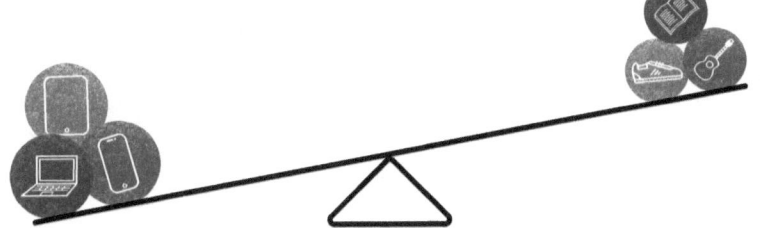

My wife is a wonderful listener. She is empathetic, intuitive, and can sense when a person is struggling, often even before they know it themselves. Kylie will sit you down, with a warm smile and open body language, and ask you a simple question, 'How are you feeling?' If people feel comfortable, they will share what they know – 'I'm tired,' 'I had a hard day at work,' 'My shoulder is playing up.' But with time and patience, my wife will often help people discover what is really going on. Her favourite question is: *'What is the thing behind the thing?'*

I like this question, for there is almost always a 'thing behind the thing' – anger at being misunderstood, shame for past mistakes, sadness for difficulties in the family. Relationships are complex because people are complex, and we bring our complexity into parenting. We parent from a set of stories and assumptions that come from our past and shape how we make decisions. Sometimes we are aware of the 'thing behind the thing', and other times we are blissfully unaware. Our beliefs and stories impact how we approach parenting, which is why there is value in examining our philosophies.

In writing this handbook I have become aware of how many assumptions I bring from my past to the present. Like you, I parent from my own perspectives, and my stories and assumptions guide the way I see the world – informed by current research. So, to set the scene and get us on the same page, let me outline three parenting philosophies – 'the thing behind the thing' – that shape my approach to tech-healthy parenting. Like any good play, my intention is to set the scene by introducing the context, establishing a storyline, and whetting your appetite for the unfolding plot.

Open curtains ...

CHAPTER 1

RAISE ADULTS, NOT CHILDREN

HEBREWS 12:1 'No discipline seems pleasant at the time, but painful. Later on, however, it produces a harvest of righteousness and peace for those who have been trained by it.'

When my first child was born, a good friend gave me some great advice. Mick encouraged me to keep my eye on the endgame because 'the role of a parent is to raise an adult, not a child'.

We live in a culture where older people are mocked and young people are worshipped. This is the reverse of many cultures around the world, and certainly most cultures throughout history. While I appreciate the importance of encouraging, celebrating and learning from youth, it's not helpful to make our children the centre of the universe. Childhood is a wonderful part of life's journey, but adulthood is the main game. Adulthood is where we spend the majority of our lives. It's how we contribute to society and leave our mark on the world. Rather than 'adulting' being an unnecessary evil that we begrudgingly enter after losing our childhood, the process of becoming an adult is worth celebrating!*

I'm not saying we should diminish the importance of childhood or prematurely propel our children into the adult world. Quite the opposite. Childhood lays the foundation for adulthood and it is vitally important that we encourage our kids to be kids with lots of time for free play, creativity, laughter and exploration in the early years. We need to safeguard our children from experiences that draw them too quickly into the adult world, away from innocence and into complexity. At the same time, let's keep the endgame in mind. If the endgame is adulthood, we need to be sowing the seeds of character development at a young age, exposing our children to risk and responsibility in age-appropriate ways. This involves outdoor adventures, challenging play, healthy boundaries and jobs like making the bed or emptying the dishwasher. Real-world challenges train and equip our kids for the adult world, building their character muscles for when they need them most.

THE IMPORTANCE OF TOUGH LOVE

Our always-easy society is promoting the opposite. We are coddling our kids and protecting them from real-world challenges like hard work and perseverance – *and at the same time*, giving them almost everything they ask online. By exposing our children to visual experiences like murder, sex, violence and greed on television, we are propelling children into

---

* In our household we don't use the term 'adulting', even in jest. In my mind, the term suggests that becoming an adult is something to avoid. Let's use language to help our children positively transition from childhood to adulthood, in age-appropriate ways, embracing the freedom and responsibilities of growing up.

the adult world far too quickly. Easy is not always better and 'yes' is not always right. If our aim is to raise children who become healthy adults, we may need to rethink some of our cultural assumptions, particularly when it comes to kids and technology.

Ultimately, raising tech-healthy humans is about tough love. In the words of Dr Karen Brooks, from *Consuming Innocence*:

> Parents should never try to be their tot's, tween's or teen's friend. That's not their job. Sharing and understanding the popular culture kids engage with does not mean becoming their best buddy. There are other people in their lives, mainly their peers, who function in that way. The role of a parent is to prepare their child for the adult world.[1]

In other words, the role of a parent is to love, mentor and equip their children with the physical, emotional and psychological experiences they need to become adults, without trying to be their best friend. This is known as 'tough love' – the willingness to suffer and absorb setbacks to prepare our kids for a better future.* It's about laying down firm but loving boundaries, forgoing what is easy in the moment for the pursuit of longer term character gains. Tough love underpins many of the tech practices outlined in this book. For as Mick said, 'the role of a parent is to raise an adult'.

---

* Tough love is really just love – emphasising the 'boundaries' aspect of loving another. It is unconditional and not punitive. Love is a feeling *and* an action. Love is gentle *and* firm. Love is tender *and* truthful. Love is both-*and*.

CHAPTER 2

A HEALTHY BRAIN FIRST

ROMANS 12:2 – 'Do not conform to the pattern of this world, but be transformed by the renewing of your mind. Then you will be able to test and approve what God's will is.'

When my grandfather was a boy, cigarettes were everywhere. Even hospitals supplied ashtrays for patients. Doctors lit up in surgical rooms, and nurses featured on cigarette ads.

We look back and wonder how our predecessors could have been so ignorant. Surely there were signs that smoking caused lung disease, even if the science was not yet clear? Then again, social pressure is powerful, and people ignore evidence. And smoking feels good in the moment.

When future generations look back at how we gave toddlers iPads, I do wonder whether they might shake their heads in a similar way. We are already aware that the steady rise in mental health disorders in young people – including anxiety, depression and self-harm – is in lockstep with the widespread uptake of interactive media. Might it be possible, then, for future generations to look back in disbelief and ponder, 'How did they not see the connection?' 'Did they really not realise that video gaming made kids irritable and emotional?' 'Did they really not see that learning and focus diminished with early screen use?' 'Did they really not understand the impacts of interactive media on the developing brain?'

THE DEVELOPING BRAIN

This is what we do know. A child's brain is not the same as an adult brain, and early exposure to digital media is not always beneficial. To understand why this is so, we must take a look at normal childhood development.

According to research, the brain is changeable.[1] In the early years, everything our children see and experience impacts how their brains develop. Every interaction is formative – the people they talk to, the games they play, the books they read – everything. Like a sponge soaking up new experiences, a developing brain grows neurons and synapses at an amazing rate, learning from what we habitually do. This growth continues throughout childhood, shifting stages in the adolescent years (where the brain enters a 'pruning and remodelling' stage to cement personality and learning). The brain is not fully developed until about the age of 25.[2] Even then, we can still learn and grow over time.

So the inputs we give a child will impact the health of their brain. This is important for us to recognise as parents.

THE UPSTAIRS AND DOWNSTAIRS BRAIN

According to Dr Daniel Siegal, a professor of psychology, the brain is like a house with an upstairs and a downstairs level.[3] The downstairs brain includes the brain stem and limbic system, located deep within the brain structure and connected to the spinal cord. Known as the 'primitive' or 'lizard' brain, the downstairs brain controls basic functions like breathing and blinking. These systems also guide our fight, flight or freeze reactions, eliciting strong emotions like fear and anger, and impulses like flinching and yelling. When the downstairs brain is in charge, we *act* before we *think*. This is essential in dangerous situations where we must act instinctively; for example, pulling our hand away from a hot stove or leaping away from an oncoming bus. But there are times when we don't want the downstairs brain to take over. These are times when we need our higher order processes to kick in, so we can demonstrate traits like patience, empathy and self-control. This is the role of the upstairs brain.

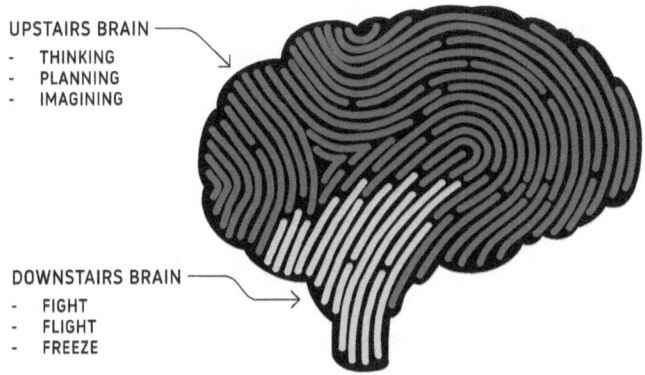

If the downstairs brain is the emotional brain, the upstairs brain is the thinking brain. It includes the cerebral cortex (the squiggly folds we see on the outside of a brain), which contains the prefrontal cortex. The upstairs brain is mature and sophisticated. It's where our higher order thinking and complex mental processing comes from, including reflecting, planning and creating. The upstairs brain can regulate the downstairs brain, but this requires energy and years of practice. It's learning to *think* before we *act*.

As you can imagine, the downstairs brain dominates early childhood because the upstairs brain is less developed. This is why children have tantrums, act on their impulses, and generally lack self-awareness and empathy. To become healthy, functioning adults, children need to mature and grow the upstairs parts of their brain. The characteristics we hope to foster in our children (associated with adulthood) are upstairs functions like patience, empathy, moral goodness, self-awareness, sound decision making and emotional control. These are not guaranteed character traits but must be fostered through love, strong relationships and experience.

We need emotional and intellectual reasoning to succeed in life, integrating the upstairs and downstairs levels in a healthy way.[4] This is why the inputs we give our children are important. They need a broad range of relational, physical and moral experiences throughout childhood to develop their upstairs brain, most of which are experienced in the real world, not on a screen.

THE PROBLEM OF OVER-STIMULATION

In a child psychiatry practice in the heart of Los Angeles, Dr Victoria Dunckley began to form a theory. It was the mid-2010s, and a steadily increasing number of children were being referred to her clinic with behavioural issues at a younger and younger age. With close observation, a pattern emerged. These children were irritable and agitated. They would have meltdowns over minor frustrations. Their school grades were falling and they struggled to keep friends because of immature behaviours. They were not excited about going outside or trying new things, and had little interest in anything other than their screens. These children had been diagnosed with a variety of conditions such as bipolar disorder and depression, but something didn't add up.

Over time, reading the clinical research, Dunckley formed a hypothesis. What if the constellation of symptoms she was seeing were not classic disorders but symptoms of electronic device overuse? What if this overuse was *causing* these dysfunctional tendencies. So she began trialling a new approach to her therapies, prescribing a structured four-week technology fast (rather than medication) for more than 500 patients over a few years. The results were immediate and incredible. There was a marked reduction in symptoms in 80% of children previously diagnosed with ADHD, bipolar disorder, depression and even psychosis, without medications.[5]

Dunckley's conclusion? Electronic media has a significant role in causing children to enter a state of hyperarousal, leading to chronic stress in the developing brain. By loading up the nervous system, children are overcooking their downstairs brain (fight or flight) and becoming dysregulated. In her words, 'screen devices interface with a child's physiological systems, altering brain chemistry, arousal level, hormones, and sleep, ultimately interfering with thinking, mood, behaviour, and social skills.'[6] Rather than tablet devices being seen as educational, Dunckley believes we should start viewing interactive media as a stimulant (like caffeine or amphetamines) because it puts children's brains into a state of hyperfocus and hyperarousal, followed by an inevitable 'crash' when the media is turned off.

The flashing colours and hyperstimulation of 'tap and swipe' devices can overstimulate the downstairs (emotional) brain and inhibit growth of the upstairs (thinking) brain. This is not a good thing in children, resulting in emotional dysregulation and a loss of learning. Recent MRI studies support Dunckley's clinical findings. For example, in the brains of internet-addicted teens, areas such as the frontal lobe – which governs planning, organising and impulse control – show grey-matter atrophy (a loss of tissue volume). The *insula*, which impacts our capacity to develop empathy and compassion for others, is damaged. A compromising of the integrity of the brain's white matter is another finding, which impacts learning by reducing the connections between various parts of the brain.[7]

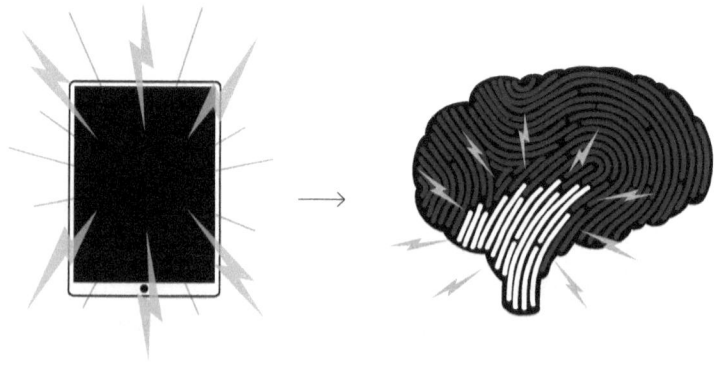

Although most such MRI studies focus on people with internet addiction, it is likely that brain damage is also occurring with lower levels of media consumption, especially in younger children.[8] According to Dr Nicholas Kardaras, one of the world's foremost addiction experts, 'brain-imaging studies conclusively show that excessive screen exposure can neurologically damage a young person's developing brain in the same way that cocaine addiction can.'[9] Think about the implications of this statement for a moment. Minecraft may equal brain cocaine in young children.[10] There is no long-term risk in *not* exposing our children to interactive media, but a mountain of evidence suggesting that early use and excessive screen exposure can result in harm.[11]

LEANING BACK OR LEANING FORWARD?

When it comes to stimulating the brain, not all forms of media are the same. Parents need to know the difference between passive and interactive media.

Long-standing media like traditional television, and streaming services like Disney Plus and Netflix, are passive in nature. We lean back and watch a story unfold on the screen. In contrast, a lot of the games and creative apps our children use are interactive. When using tablets, smartphones or gaming consoles, we lean forward because we are part of the play. Interactive media is incredibly appealing because we get to control what is happening in the story. It's also more intense for developing brains. There are flashing colours, intermittent rewards, social feedback cues and other functions intentionally designed to keep us immersed and engaged. The aim is to hyperstimulate the brain and keep children engaged with continuous novelty, releasing dopamine (a feel-good neurotransmitter) and stimulating a downstairs-brain emotional response, to keep them coming back for more.[12] If we can swipe it, or change the story, or tell it what to do, it's interactive, whether the content is 'educational' or entertaining.

Ironically, many parents monitor their children's use of passive technology because they see simply watching a screen as laziness. But these parents are often less concerned about how much time their children are spending on interactive activities because they believe these are educational. In contrast, David Murrow, author of *Drowning in Screen Time*, gives this recommendation: 'Parents should sharply restrict lean-forward screen time because of its potential to overstimulate the brain but allow their children a carefully monitored amount of lean-back screen use as appropriate.'[13] Interestingly, when children become accustomed to interactive media, they begin using passive media the same way. Just watch how teenagers skip the slower parts of a movie – while texting! If you want to reduce the mental stimulation of a movie, your children can watch it on a passive television screen rather than a phone, tablet or laptop.

Examples of passive (lean back) screen activities are:

- watching traditional TV
- streaming shows
- going to a movie
- talking on video chat with people you know.

Examples of interactive (lean forward) screen activities are:

- video gaming
- web surfing
- social media
- texting and instant messaging.

Of course, there are times when interactive media can be beneficial. When one of our children struggled to keep up with reading in school, we purchased an app to boost his literacy skills. We have encouraged our children to learn to touch type using software, and more recently, to develop coding and block-based programming skills. But we encourage passive screen-time for entertainment.

It's all about getting the right balance between the devices, the types of apps and the amount of time spent. Recognise the inherent risks embedded in lean-forward technologies and introduce them thoughtfully and in moderation.

NEAR WORK OR DISTANT WORK?

When I was a boy, my father warned me that watching television would give me 'square eyes'. This was tongue in cheek, but mobile devices can impact the visual health of children. The problem is not with blue light emitted from screens but how far away we hold our devices from our eyes. Phones, tablets and laptops are smaller and therefore viewed closer than television screens, typically less than 40 centimetres from our faces. By increasing 'near work' we are increasing near-sightedness (called myopia). This is no small issue. The World Health Organization estimates that half of the world's population will be myopic by 2050 – impacted by our ubiquitous use of screens and reduced time spent outdoors.[14]

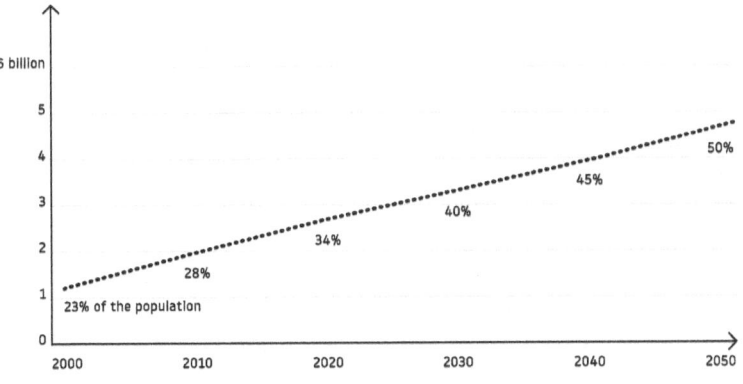

PROJECTED NUMBER OF PEOPLE WITH NEAR-SIGHTEDNESS WORLDWIDE

Data sourced from B.A. Holden et al, 2016, *Journal of American Academy of Opthamology*

When people are near-sighted they can see close up but not far away. We can compensate with glasses, but extreme myopia is a serious health problem. A person with a prescription of more than six corrective units has an increased risk of retinal detachment, cataracts, glaucoma and ocular diseases that impact vision. In fact, there is a 90% likelihood of a person with extreme myopia becoming visually impaired by the age of 75.[15] I am not saying that using tablets will make your children lose their eyesight – genetic factors and outdoor time are significant – but 'near work' can be a factor and worth monitoring in children.

The visual system, like the brain, is plastic and therefore sensitive to environmental factors in the early years of development. Studies from China, Taiwan, Denmark and Ireland found an increase in myopia in children who participated in online learning during lockdown. In one study, six-year-old children who participated in online learning for several months were three times more likely to be near-sighted than their counterparts. The risk lowered with age – eight-year-old children were 1.4 times more likely and older children had no statistically significant differences in vision.[16] Once again, the younger the child, the more considerate we need to be of interactive near-work.

As such, according to paediatric ophthalmologist Dr Rupa Wong, television is better than handheld devices. This is because 'distant targets' are better than 'near targets' for developing eyes. Here are her recommendations:

- Where possible, save your child's 'near work' for reading and writing, rather than entertainment.
- Encourage your children to watch television with the screen 1.5 to 2 metres from their eyes.
- Encourage regular time outdoors because sunlight is essential for visual health.
- When your children do participate in 'near work', encourage the 20-20 rule*: pausing every 20 minutes to look in the distance for 20 seconds.[17]

---

* The 20-20 rule is about reducing eye fatigue and dry eyes, and is a good habit for adults and children alike. But it won't reduce the development of near-sightedness in children at risk of myopia.

THE LEADERS OF TOMORROW WILL NEED HEALTHY BRAINS

While there is no 'right' approach to parenting, we should be thoughtful about how quickly we introduce interactive media to children. There is limited and contradictory data about whether some apps or games have educational benefits.[18] There is a growing body of evidence linking internet overuse with brain dysregulation in children.[19,20] The best way to prepare a child for adulthood is to do what we have always done: spend time with them engaging in activities that enhance the upstairs brain, such as being outdoors, playing with loved ones and being physically active.

Let's teach our kids how to think clearly and regulate their emotions before exposing them to hyperstimulating technologies, for the leaders of tomorrow will need a fully functioning brain. They will need the ability to concentrate, problem solve, sleep soundly, be resilient, work alongside others and control their impulses. There is no shortcut to developing a healthy brain and visual system. We need loving relationships, creative play, adventures, physical books, imaginative games, and a series of broad and diverse experiences to develop the upstairs brain. We even need some boredom for our brains to wander and learn to be creative.

In the words of Dr Nicholas Kardaras: 'People need to first fully develop their brains – their cognitive, attentional, linguistic, emotional, spatial and reality-testing mental faculties – before their brains can go beyond those areas and handle hyper arousing and reality-immersing screens.'[21] Step one. Develop a healthy brain. Step two. Add technology.*

---

* There are pre-conditions for the development of a healthy brain in infants and young children, including a safe and secure environment (physical and emotional), loving relationships and opportunities for exploration.

If we want our children to get a head start in creativity, numeracy and literacy, the evidence is clear. Read them physical books. Get them outdoors. Talk with them during meals. Engage in play that uses body language and eye contact. Help them be physically active.

Start with a healthy brain.

CHAPTER 3

LIFE-GIVING LIMITS

MATTHEW 7:13 'Enter through the narrow gate. For wide is the gate and broad is the road that leads to destruction, and many enter through it.'

Many of us think about limits in a negative way. Boundaries feel oppressive. We worry they will take away our autonomy and self-expression. But in reality, the opposite is true. We all need limits. Limits are life giving, for when aligned with reality, limits expand personal freedom and increase health and happiness. This is true for both adults and children.

Think about money. If we have no limits and spend everything we earn on consumer goods, the result is not more freedom. We end up with financial stress and long-term debt, missing out on the benefits of accumulated wealth later in life. Wise people make voluntary choices to constrain their spending to save for the future. The result is greater financial freedom and a better quality of life. The same is true in almost every area of personal development. Want to live a long and healthy life? Limit your alcohol and calorie intake. Want to stay safe on the road? Limit your speed. Want to avoid burn out? Limit how much time you spend at work, and prioritise sleep.

Everything works this way. Boundaries can improve our quality of life, including digital boundaries.

The same is true for our children. 'Time to go to bed,' to ensure enough sleep. 'Don't leave the lights on,' to contain our electricity costs. 'Only one scoop of ice-cream,' to limit the blood sugar levels of our already hyperactive kids. The list goes on and on.

But here's the problem: we have not yet translated the logic of limits to our use of screens. In the timeline of human history, screen use is unbelievably new. The television is less than a hundred years old. Personal computers are about half this age. And tablets, barely teenagers! We are struggling to understand the importance of screen limits as a society because our digital landscape is so new and changing quickly.

WHAT ARE THE APPROPRIATE BOUNDARIES?

According to the national guidelines for screen time in Australia, children under two years old should not be exposed to screens at all. Children between two and five years old should have a maximum of one hour of screen time a day. Young people aged five to seventeen years should limit screen use to two hours a day (excluding activities for study or work.)[1,2] This is not just good advice. It's based on the best evidence to date around the world. The younger the child, the more screen vigilant we should be.

In reality, not many parents are following these guidelines, either because they are unaware, or feel overwhelmed by the complexities of life. I understand how hard it can be to minimise screen time in a tech-soaked culture. Some of us rely on the 'electronic babysitter' to finish our work, or cook dinner, or take a breath after a hectic day. There are unique challenges with single parenting, and shift work, and parenting a disabled child, making every situation unique. Even so, let's try our best to follow these guidelines. Be kind on yourself when you stuff up, but don't miss by a country mile.

0 - 2 YEARS OLD	2 - 5 YEARS OLD	5 - 17 YEARS OLD
NIL	1 HOUR PER DAY	2 HOUR PER DAY + STUDY / WORK

Clearly it's important to avoid violent or sexually explicit content, but we must also be conscious of how the content is being viewed. Remember leaning back and leaning forward? The more interactive and hyper-intense a media experience, the more cautious we should be. A research study of 2000 kindergarten, primary school and junior high school children found that sleep disturbance occurred with just 30 minutes of interactive media (computer games) compared with two hours of passive (television) use.[3] So it's not just about screen time but the devices used.

For babies, toddlers and preschool children, you may want to treat your phone and tablet like dangerous chemicals in the cupboard. When your child reaches out to play with your phone, give them a kind but firm 'no', just as you would if they found strong cleaning chemicals under the sink. For while it may be cute to see your baby swipe an app on your phone – 'look how clever they are!' – it creates a snowball effect, setting up the expectation that these devices are fair game. This makes it harder to establish better boundaries later.

If your toddler already regularly uses a phone or tablet, take heart. There's plenty of time to recalibrate things. It just means you may need to work a bit harder to implement healthier strategies and expect a bit more push-back in the process. My hope is to give you practical advice to help you strengthen the social, emotional and physical health of your children as you guide their tech habits.

GET CREATIVE IN HOW YOU SET LIMITS

When our children were young, we set clear limits on when and how often they could use a screen. They always watched television together, using a monitor rather than a laptop or tablet. They had consistent screen-free days.

But things started to change when they reached the pre-teen years. They began to complain that our approach was too controlling and wanted more autonomy in what they watched and when. So we implemented what we call 'the token system'.[4] Rather than telling our children when they could or could not watch television, we gave them five hours a week of screen time and asked them to monitor themselves. To do this, they received 10 tokens a week, with each token worth 30 minutes of screen time. We monitored usage to ensure they were being honest. We taught them strategies (such as setting a timer) to help them accurately keep track of their behaviours. We also created guardrails: they could use a maximum of two hours of tokens per day, and none before breakfast or after dinner on weekdays. This worked well for many years because it allowed our children to choose when they watched television, giving them more autonomy. It helped them to begin self-monitoring their use of screens, an essential skill for the teen years.

Over time, the token system has changed along with our family. Our children asked us if they could earn tokens by doing extra jobs around the house. This seemed reasonable, and it has helped us get a lot of washing and cleaning done over the years! The negative and unintended consequence is that our children have come to value screen time like money, with tokens being a reward for good behaviour.

Another shift is our children now watch programs on individual laptops, rather than together. This drift largely happened because of our time in COVID-19 lockdowns. After experiencing remote learning, we agreed to give them additional screen time 'academic' tokens (for coding, maths and creative writing), which drifted towards individual screen use. Now our children predominantly watch programs on their own devices rather than together. I miss watching shared programs as a family, but I also acknowledge the need for self-expression as they get older.

As many parents experience, we are finding it harder to keep an eye on what our children are watching now they use laptops for school. The line between 'homework' and 'play' is blurry, making it harder to navigate healthy screen-time limits. Like all things parenting, some days we feel like we're making big mistakes, and other times we're amazed at the maturity and thoughtfulness of our children. We keep learning and adapting, willing to reset what we do as circumstances change.

A POSITIVE REFRAME

Screen time limits are important and we can approach the logic of limits with a positive reframe. Our intention is not to *restrict* but to *reclaim*! When we say 'no' to excessive screens we must always keep in mind the greater 'yes.'[5] Are we fixating on what we are taking away, or focusing on the benefits of a life lived more expansively beyond screens?

Limits can be life-giving when established in love. So rather than feeling guilty for denying our children time online, let's celebrate the symphony of life unplugged.

As we end this section and move to part II, I encourage you to keep these three parenting foundations in the back of your mind:

- We're raising adults, not children.
- We're developing a healthy brain before adding interactive technologies.
- We're setting life-giving limits to embrace free play, expressive boredom, generative relationships and other meaningful activities away from a screen.

With these principles in place, it's time to explore the STARTER Framework.

Below are three questions to help you stop, reflect and gain the most from what you have explored.

What *three significant insights* have arisen from what you have read so far?

What *two practical actions* will you commit to doing soon?

What *one big question* do you still have?

PART II
THE STARTER FRAMEWORK

When my wife became pregnant with our first child, we didn't find out their sex in advance. Rather than talk about our unborn baby as a 'boy' or 'girl', we affectionately named them 'Dumpling'. Continuing the Asian street-food tradition, our second child became 'Wonton'. When our third child was conceived, it would have been logical to call them 'Noodle' or 'Spring roll' or 'Moon cake', but we didn't. We referred to them as 'Slartibartfast'.

I know this is strange. Slartibartfast is the name of a planetary architect in *The Hitchhiker's Guide to the Galaxy*, and I have no idea why we started using it.[1] When our baby finally entered the world, our friends decided to round off the joke by giving us a present. It was a tiny jumpsuit with two words printed on it: 'Don't Panic!' For those who are less nerdy than me, 'Don't Panic' features on the cover of the *Hitchhiker's Guide to the Galaxy*, apparently to prevent intergalactic travellers from freaking out. While it's good advice for space travellers, it's essential advice for parents seeking to raise tech-healthy humans in the digital age.

In this section of the book, we'll explore seven digital parenting strategies to help you set up your kids for life. This section is ordered in a logical, step-by-step manner to help you make wise decisions along your tech parenting journey. My hope is to provide you with enough information to keep you moving, but not so much as to overwhelm you.

In writing this framework, I acknowledge that no formula can address the many complexities of parenting in the digital age. There will be nuances in how these ideas are applied in various contexts; for example, in mixed-race marriages, blended families, and households struggling with financial stress. There is no ABC guide to raising perfect children – you can do all the right things and still end up with a wayward teenager, and vice versa.

That said, everyone can gain something from the STARTER Framework. When reading this section, ask yourself the question – *what applies to me and my situation?* What can I apply next? If you feel overwhelmed, you can always put the book down, take a breath, and remember there is no perfect parent. You can even imagine yourself wearing a comfortable adult-sized jumpsuit emblazoned with the slogan, *'Don't Panic!'*

Here is the framework:

- **S**tart with self
- **T**ake it slowly
- **A**ge-appropriate setup
- **R**egular talk
- **T**ech-health rhythms
- **E**ncourage adventures
- **R**ely on others

The STARTER Framework is about giving your children a great start to life in an always-on culture. There are seven chapters in this part, building on one another. Read them quickly or slowly, and whatever you do, *don't panic*. Parenting is hard work, and by reading this book you're already ahead of the game. If you implement just one or two ideas from this framework, that's a huge win.

Let's get started.

CHAPTER 4

START WITH SELF

COR 11:1 'Follow my example, as I follow the example of Christ.'

I was in Sydney training a group of leaders on how to make space in their busy lives. A lady started to tear up and was clearly struggling with the content of my presentation, so I stopped and made space to hear what she was thinking and feeling. Bravely she shared what was on her mind: 'I find technology really hard. I'm a mum with young children, and in my head I just want to be present and give them my undivided time and attention. But all I feel like is checking my latest Instagram post to see how many "hearts" I'm getting. I think I have a problem.'

I really appreciated this lady's honesty, particularly in front of her peers. While I don't struggle with social media myself, I do wrestle with compulsively checking Gmail and doom-scrolling the news. Almost all of us struggle with digital overload in some way, especially parents who are tired and overwhelmed. When our home becomes a storm of messy toys and temper tantrums, any escape can feel like a welcome relief – including hiding in cyberspace. This is fine in moderation – so long as it doesn't detract from real life. But if our compulsive screen behaviours start to negatively impact those we love, including ourselves, we may need to get honest. We may need to shine a light on our own technology behaviours – to *start with self*.

It's easy to complain about our children's dysfunctional tech habits. But it takes guts to hold a mirror to self and admit we may have a problem. The tech behaviours we model to our children will invariably shape their habits and values. If, for example, we tell our children to put away their tablets as we zone out on the couch scrolling Facebook, what message are we sending? In the famous words of Ralph Waldo Emerson, 'What you do speaks so loudly that I cannot hear what you say.'[1] This is why the STARTER Framework begins with self-examination, for our parenting actions speak louder than our words.

Am I being the kind of adult that I want my children to be?

BEHAVIOUR IS AN OUTWORKING OF BELIEF

Human behaviour is an outworking of belief – the things we believe to be true about ourselves and the world around us. Like an iceberg rising above the water, our habits are often visible to all, but the stories and narratives guiding our behaviours are hidden below the surface. It is possible to alter our stories but this takes practice – the willingness to examine the fears, needs and insecurities that motivate our actions. This is why we start with self, for unless we shift our beliefs we cannot sustain meaningful behaviour change.

Let me give you an example related to digital technology.

In my previous book, I shared a simple idea: turn off your phone and devices for one day each week to rest your mind and refresh your relationships. We don't need a lot of information to give this a go – just slide to power off and put your devices in the cupboard. Easy! In reality, unplugging for a full day is not easy. It is incredibly hard to do. Just the idea of being offline for a full day can make some people panic. Why is this? It's because of our stories!

Unplugging is painful because our devices help us to express the deeper values and purposes of our lives. When our phones become a part of our *identity*, an extension of ourselves, switching off becomes unfathomable. If, for example, career and achievement are where we find our self-worth, logging off the internet is not an option. What if we were to miss an email? What if this held up a project? We *need* to be seen as hard working, even on our days off – always producing and achieving something important, because of our story. If, in contrast, we find self-worth in approval from others, unplugging is illogical because we might let people down. What if we missed a text? What if our friends thought we were ghosting them? So we can't disconnect because we believe that missing a message would damage our reputation and, ultimately, our self-worth.

These are just a few examples of the stories we tell ourselves. Now, of course, a person doesn't have to answer weekend emails to be a valuable employee, or respond to a message immediately to be a lovable friend. But it's hard to convince ourselves to use logic when we're working from illogical narratives.

BEHAVIOUR NEVER LIES

The life scripts that shape our behaviours are often hidden from plain sight. According to insecurity expert Jaemin Frazer, 'behaviour never lies'.[2] Humans behave in certain ways, for particular reasons, and what we *do* on a repetitive basis can help us discover what we *believe* about the world and ourselves.

He explains that every behaviour is simply an attempt to meet our needs or protect our fears. 'Behaviour never lies' means that a person can work backwards to understand why they act the way they do by asking, 'What must I believe about myself in order to behave this way?'

For example, if you habitually email late at night when you don't have to, that's something objective to work with. You can ask yourself a few probing questions to uncover your hidden motives. Why do I check email compulsively? What meaning or rewards do I get out of this? Comfort? Security? Self-worth? What does working late at night say about my identity? How do my habits benefit me? How have I come to see the world in this way?

Our habits exist for a reason. Behaviours never lie. We can ask reflective questions to uncover our hidden motivations and values, for both the digital and non-digital aspects of our lives. Why do I eat when I'm stressed? Why can't I take a day off? Why do I feel angry when my father-in-law is in town? Why do I check my phone on the toilet? Why do I habitually check the news when it makes me upset? Why do I watch YouTube when I'm bored? Why do I …

BE THE ADULT YOU WANT YOUR CHILDREN TO BE

Self-reflection takes courage. It can be confronting and painful to look in the mirror and examine your inner life. The process can open up memories or emotions and require that you reach out for support from people you trust. You may even need professional guidance to help you process some of what you find. But the payoff is enormous. For to be a healthier human is to be a healthier parent. In the words of shame-resilience author Brené Brown, 'Who we are and how we engage with the world are much stronger predictors of how our children will do than what we know about parenting.'[3] We can learn everything there is to know about raising children, but if we don't care for ourselves, forgive our own mistakes or experience a sense of peace in our inner lives, how can we teach these qualities to our children? If we don't approach our own mistakes with honesty and vulnerability, how will we teach our children to do the same?

I'm not saying we must have everything under control – quite the opposite. We just need the integrity to start with self – tackling our own illogical digital habits and behaviours before trying to help others around us.*

THE SILVER LINING

So, we agree we have a problem? That's fantastic news! Self-awareness is the beginning of personal transformation. If you are willing to look in the mirror and bravely accept your need to shift your own digital habits then you are on the right path.

Here's the good news: you don't have to wait until you have it 'all together' before attempting to tackle your family's online behaviours. Our struggles and mistakes are hidden opportunities if we choose to see them this way. Can you bring your children on the journey with you? This is the silver lining. Even our mistakes can enable positive change in the ones we love.

Let's say, for example, you have been modelling unhelpful digital work behaviours at home. Rather than being present with

---

* If you need more support to do this, please read my previous book *Spacemaker*, which is full of practical advice about how to shift our digital paradigms, principles and practices as adults.

your family or engaging as your tweens get ready for school, you're on your phone, answering emails and getting distracted. It's chaos. Everyone is always rushed and frazzled in the morning. No one is focused. Invariably someone yells or has a meltdown as you all rush out the door. Worse still, you realise your kids have copied your bad habits. Rather than making lunches or preparing for the day, they spend the morning on their laptops checking Spotify or messaging friends. Things would improve if you could all be present and focused.

Gulp. Time to change things up.

Now you have a few options. You can yell at your children. You can feel bad about your situation and give up. Or you can be creative and model vulnerability by asking your family to help you find a solution together:

> Hey kids. I've been thinking about our morning routine and how we're always rushing out the door. I'm sorry for my part in this. I've been distracted and unavailable, checking work emails instead of helping us get ready. I'm particularly aware of how much our phones and devices are distracting us from being organised in the morning. I think it'd be fantastic if we could change up our habits and be more organised together. How about we try no devices before we leave the house on weekdays so we're not in such a rush? Could we make this change together. Are you willing to go on this journey with me? Here's an idea! If I stuff up you can keep me accountable. Heck, if I reach for my phone before you head to school, you can fine me $5. But I expect you to work on this alongside me. What do you think? Deal?

I'm not guaranteeing this will work, but if you want to reset your own tech habits, there's value in doing this as a family. 'Sorry, I made a mistake' is a better approach than 'Stop goofing around and get ready for school!' There is power in collective change. There is wisdom in 'we' – 'I think **we** have a problem and how can **we** work on this together?'

There are so many tough decisions that come our way as our children progress through the stages of life from tots, to tweens, to teens and beyond. By continually examining self we grow our capacity to change, responding appropriately as our children change. This is especially important at milestone points in the journey, like when we find ourselves confronted by questions such as, 'when do I get my child their first phone?' – the focus of our next chapter.

IN SUM

- Parenting is less about *what we know* and more about *who we are*. This is because healthier humans make healthier parents, so we start with self.

- We all struggle with digital overuse at different times in our lives and need the bravery to shine a light on our own habits.

- 'Actions speak louder than words', and the tech habits we model to our children will inevitably shape what they do.

- 'Behaviour is an outworking of belief', which means that our digital habits are influenced by our stories and beliefs.

- 'Behaviour never lies', which means we can work backwards to discover why we do what we do, asking 'what must I believe about myself in order to behave this way?' Sometimes our unconscious beliefs are hard to detect, and we may need professional support to help us move forward.

- Unhelpful digital habits can be an opportunity to grow together as a family. Consider this approach: 'I think **we** have a problem and how can **we** work on this together?'

SOMETHING TO THINK ABOUT

What is one digital habit that you would like to shift in your own life to model better behaviours for your children?

CHAPTER 5

TAKE IT SLOWLY

PROVERBS 22:6 'Start children off on the way they should go, and even when they are old they will not turn from it.'

One of the most common questions I am asked is, 'When should I get my child their first phone?' It seems this is no longer a question of 'if' but 'when'.*

Here are some statistics:

- One in three Australian children will have a smartphone by age 12.[1]
- The average age of receiving a smartphone is 7.7 years old.[2]
- In Australia, 94% of teens between 14 and 17 have a smartphone.[3]

---

* I have used the terms 'phone' and 'smartphone' interchangeably, as these days 'phone' almost always means 'smartphone'. I discuss the role of 'dumb phones' (no internet) in a later chapter.

Put another way, only 6% of teenagers *do not* have a smartphone. And by the time I publish this book, these statistics will have shifted again. While the majority of children do not yet own their own phone, many do. We are steamrolling towards a ubiquitous uptake of mobile devices in primary school, with children as young as six years old getting their own phones.

Interestingly, many of the leaders of Silicon Valley tech companies do not give technology to their children as readily as we do. This is well documented but worth repeating. Steve Jobs was hesitant to give his children an iPad, preferring to talk at the dinner table about history and literature.[4] Sundar Pichai, CEO of Google, limits his phone and computer use and strictly monitors his family's screen time. The co-founder and CEO of Snapchat, Evan Spiegel, once commented that his stepson was restricted to 90 minutes of screen time a week.[5] And Sean Parker, the founding president of Facebook, who is now a conscientious objector of the technologies he helped create, controversially stated: 'God only knows what it's doing to our children's brains!'[6]

If Silicon Valley's elite are cautious about how early they adopt technology with their own children, we should pay attention. While it can be good to be an early adopter, technology and children is one area where we must go slow – particularly when giving children their own smartphones.

WHY WE GIVE PHONES TO YOUNG CHILDREN

When speaking with parents in schools, I come across three common reasons why parents are giving smartphones to their pre-teens:

- I want my child to be safe.
- They keep nagging and it is hard to say 'no'.
- Devices are educational.

In each of these situations, parents have absorbed a story told to them by popular culture, compelling them to give their children phones far too early in their development. Each of these stories is a fable lacking in evidence, not a truth.

Let me tackle these myths one at a time.

MYTH 1: PHONES MAKE OUR CHILDREN SAFER

Something happened in the 1980s that changed how my parents felt about safety. A young boy named Richard Kelvin was abducted, held captive, drugged and murdered in Adelaide, my hometown. He was dragged into a car just 300 metres from his home. It was terrifying. Richard was the son of a popular television news presenter, Rob Kelvin, who we watched every night at 6pm. Our hearts broke collectively as we saw the visible pain of this boy's death in his father's eyes.[7]

This tragic incident transformed our community. Rather than being allowed to walk to school, parents began walking their children to the bus stop to keep them close by. Neighbourhood collectives formed to provide safe houses. The government launched an educational campaign to warn us of stranger danger. So rather than trusting the person next door, every unknown person became a potential threat.

Culture changes slowly, for various reasons. Fifty years on, we have become a hyper-vigilant society around children and safety, influenced by events like the one above. Many of these changes are good and helpful, but some are irrational and driven by fear. Child abductions are – and have always been – extremely rare. And while Adelaide has been unfairly tainted as the 'murder capital' of Australia, because of a handful of bizarre serial homicides, it is one of the safest cities in the world. But every time something happens to a child, here or abroad, we hear about it. We watch global news and feel personally concerned. So we give our children smartphones. *Just in case.*

Smartphones actually introduce our children to more danger

Ironically, while rates of murder and armed robbery have decreased since the 1990s in Australia (as well as in America), teen suicide is at an all-time high.[8] Suicide is now the leading cause of death among Australians aged 15 to 24 years old.[9] Since the widespread adoption of smartphones, mental health issues in young people have increased, leading to what can only be described as an epidemic of anxiety, depression and suicide. Mental health is complicated and influenced by many factors, but a picture is emerging, with research linking mental health problems with unhelpful online behaviours in pre-teens and teens.[10]

According to Chris McKenna, founder of Protect Young Eyes, we are overly concerned about the risk of physical danger imposed by strangers and blind to the actual dangers our children are experiencing online through cyberbullying, pornography and online grooming. Here are some Australian statistics:

- more than 50% of young people have experienced cyberbullying[11]
- nearly 50% of young people are regularly exposed to sexually explicit content[12, 13]
- 30% of Australian teens have been contacted by a stranger on the internet.[14]

In McKenna's words, 'We have put little boxes of porn in our children's pockets, under the guise of safety, under the guise of protection, and the guise that I need to be in touch with my child all the time every day.'[15] So the question must be asked, do smartphones really make our children safer? Or do they only make us *feel* safer (which is not at all the same thing).

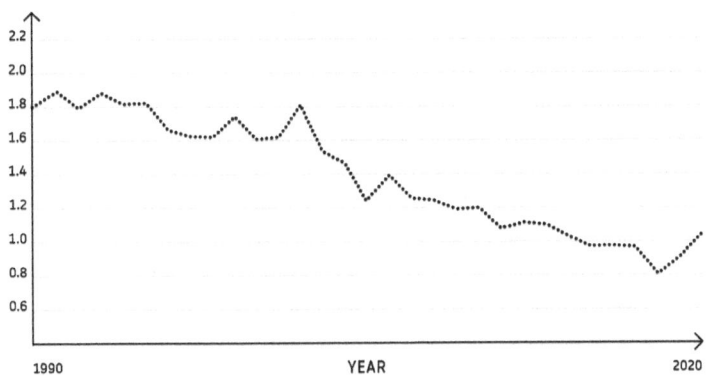

Data sourced from Australian Institute of Criminology, Australian Government.

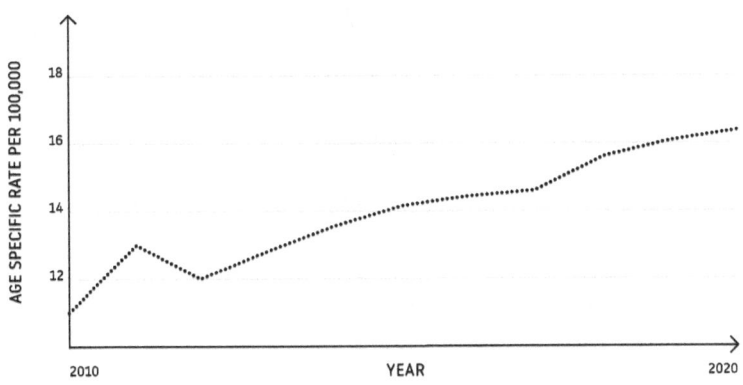

Data sourced from Australian Institute of Health and Welfare, Australian Government.

MYTH 2: SAYING 'YES' WILL STOP MY CHILD NAGGING

Nagging is exhausting. It wears us down. In spite of our good intentions, it can be hard to say 'no' and then hold our ground. Especially when there is so much external pressure to give our children what they want – their very own phone – at a younger and younger age.

Here are just a few of the many pressures that squeeze families in the pre-teen years:

- **Consumer pressure:** Children are targeted by a multi-billion-dollar marketing industry, led by psychologists and behavioural experts, designed to secure a purchase.
- **School pressure:** As more schools adopt 'bring your own devices' and 'iPad as reward' policies, it becomes harder to say 'no' at home. My children first played Minecraft in the classroom, and a host of other so-called 'educational' games. I acknowledge there may be legitimate reasons for using interactive devices in the classroom, but it makes parenting harder at home.
- **Peer pressure:** When my oldest child first expressed that 'everyone at school has a phone', I dismissed her claims abruptly. Susan didn't have a phone. Tod didn't have a phone. Jenna didn't have a phone. Her statement wasn't true. Six years later, when my youngest child bemoaned the same thing, he had evidence backing his claim. Many of his friends did have a phone and it was harder to deny his request for one. As parents, we want the best for our children. No one likes feeling left out in the playground. No one wants to be picked last on the soccer team. When your child becomes one of the last

kids in their class to get a device, it feels harder to hold your ground, particularly if it's impacting their social life. It may require honest, creative conversations and the ability to take the long view.

Remember this: giving your pre-teen a smartphone will not stop them nagging. If anything, it creates **more** nagging. By exposing your child to targeted advertising, including the echo chamber of social media, they see more, they want more, they ask for more. And if nagging worked the first time, guess what happens next? More nagging! 'Can I have Snapchat?' 'Can I have TikTok?' 'Why can't I watch horror movies like my friends?' It never ends. At some point, as engaged parents, we need the willingness to set life-giving boundaries for our children. That means saying 'no'. Full stop. To refuse to set limits and hold your ground is to relinquish your parenting responsibilities to Silicon Valley tech companies. Trust me. They do not love your children as much as you do.

It's hard to set boundaries and allow children to cry when they don't get what they want. But in my experience, nagging only reduces when we set well-considered boundaries and follow through. This begins at a young age: 'I don't want to eat my vegetables', 'I don't want to say sorry', 'I don't want to go to sleep'. Remember, tough love is about making hard choices in the moment to raise adults with good character.* In our family, nagging is not an acceptable behaviour. We made a decision

---

* One of Jordan Peterson's '12 Rules For Life' is, 'Do not let your children do anything that makes you dislike them.' In Peterson's thinking, our duty as parents is to make our children socially desirable, because this is necessary to thrive in the adult world. Nagging is not a behavioural trait that is tolerable in the workplace and therefore shouldn't be acceptable at home.

early in our family to treat nagging like disobedience, setting consequences for ongoing misbehaviour. Rather than being rewarded, our children would miss out on privileges like screen time if they whined or complained. We explained they were missing out because of their behaviour. At the same time, we try to say 'yes' as much as possible and encourage our children to be forthright in asking for what they want using rational arguments and a calm tone of voice (which is altogether different to nagging).

'No' and 'not yet' are unavoidable parts of parenting. Loving boundaries protect children and set them on the right path. Getting your child a smartphone will not stop them nagging. So lovingly hold your ground.

MYTH 3: PHONES INCREASE EDUCATIONAL OUTCOMES

There has been much written on this subject, so I will be brief.

Technology has often been touted as the panacea of education, but the reality is different. Study after study has failed to demonstrate the educational benefits of using technology in classrooms. In contrast, multiple studies have concluded that students learn the foundations of reading, writing and mathematics best when using analogue methods. This is particularly true in schools where children struggle with numeracy and literacy. When technology is introduced in schools that already perform to a high standard there can be a marginal gain, but the impact on learning outcomes in average or below average schools is neutral and often detrimental. Simply put, great teachers create great education, and when technology is adopted by average and below average teachers it is a distraction.[16]

Again, this is not a debate about the benefits of technology per se, but the age at which it is introduced in a child's learning journey. According to educational expert Joseph Chilton Pearce, 'we must encourage children to develop the ability to think first, and then give them the computer. After that, the sky's the limit. But if you introduce the computer before the child's thought processes are worked out, then you have a disaster in the making.'[17]

So don't be pressured by academic myths. Your child will not miss out on university because they don't own a phone in primary school. More likely, they will rise above the pack by not spending as much time online as their peers. With less swiping, scrolling and gaming, your child has a better chance of developing a healthy mind. Let's teach them how to read, sleep and concentrate before introducing highly addictive media into the mix.

By slowing down with technology, we set them up for success.

SO, WHAT SHOULD YOU DO?

The question remains, 'When should I get my child their first smartphone?'

I wish I could give you a definitive answer. Different children have different personalities. Different families have different values. Different communities create different social pressures. There is no one size fits all.

But here is what I do recommend: *go as slowly as possible*. Don't be an early adopter in this situation. Go slower than the world around you. I suggest avoiding phones until high school, or better still, mid-to-late high school if you can.* Push comes to shove, the decision to give your child a phone is as much about your readiness as theirs. You will know the time is right to give *your* child a phone when *you* are ready to have the difficult conversations that follow this decision. In the profound words of parenting author Julianna Miner, 'If you're not comfortable discussing porn on the internet with your kid, then either you're not ready to get them a phone or they're not ready to have one.'[18] This is very wise. Is your child emotionally, mentally and spiritually mature enough to dive into this adult world? And are you ready to dive in with them?

If so, the time may be right to give them a smartphone.

Whatever you decide to do, don't be pressured by others. You are the one who gets to choose when your child receives their first phone. Not Apple. Not your school. Not your child's best friend. Be brave. Be thoughtful. Be informed. You can be the hero of your child's story by wisely waiting until the time is right.

What if the ship has sailed? What if you have invertedly dived in too quickly and need to reset? Or alternatively, what if after reading this chapter you decide it really *is* time to get your child a phone. How might you go about this in a sensible way?

Let's find out!

---

* In his extensively researched book *The Anxious Generation*, Jonathan Haidt proposes four foundational reforms to improve our children's mental health and wellbeing. These are: 1) No smartphones before high school; 2) No social media before 16; 3) Phone-free schools, and 4) Far more unsupervised play and childhood independence. Given the growing research linking social media and smartphone use to reduced adolescent mental health, I endorse these recommendations.

IN SUM

- There is tremendous pressure to give children smartphones at a young age. But the leaders of Silicon Valley tech companies take a more cautious approach with their own children, giving us reason to pause.

- We rationalise the need to give children a phone in three ways: a) phones make our children safer; b) saying 'yes' will stop them nagging; c) phones are educational. These myths are contrary to evidence.

- Although there is no definitive answer to, 'When should I get my child their first phone,' a good rule of thumb is to *go as slowly as possible*. Remember that smartphones open up our children to the adult world.

- The question we need to ask is not only 'are they ready' but 'am I ready?' Am I ready to talk with my child about adult issues such as online pornography? And are they ready?

- You get to decide when and how you give your child their first phone. Hold your ground if you can. Be the hero of your child's story.

> **SOMETHING TO THINK ABOUT**
>
> Would you give your child nude adult pictures or encourage them to talk with strangers without supervision? How does this influence your decision about how early you give your child a smartphone?

CHAPTER 6

AGE-APPROPRIATE SETUP

2 THESSALONIANS 3:3 'But the Lord is faithful, and he will strengthen you and protect you from the evil one.'

I regularly chop and split wood on a property we own. One day my nine-year-old son was watching me chainsaw a fallen log. I could see he was curious, and so I asked him if he wanted to learn how to use a chainsaw. He was tentative but said 'yes'. We sat down and I gave him a lesson about how to use a chainsaw safely. We practised using the handbrake, keeping his wrist in position. I gave him safety glasses, ear muffs and a face shield. I set up a medium-sized log for him to work on, pulled the cord and let her rip.

My wide-eyed son took hold of the powerful tool.

But rather than enjoying the experience, he made one cut and put the chainsaw down, clearly rattled. He didn't have the upper body strength to control or bear the weight of the chainsaw. He struggled, and it scared him. He felt afraid when woodchips started flying towards him. He found the experience difficult and demotivating. This was a wakeup call for me as a dad. I realised, afresh, how small my boy was and how strong I am in comparison.

Children are not adults. Some tools are simply too powerful for kids to handle safely.

In the previous chapter we explored when to give your child their first smartphone. Now it's time to discuss how to set up your child's phone in an age-appropriate way. For like a chainsaw, a smartphone is an incredibly powerful tool.* A single smartphone has enough processing power to guide a self-driving car, monitor chemical warfare attacks or navigate a rocket to the moon. In the words of Jordan Foster, child psychologist and founder of YSafe: 'Never give a child a phone as it is. All phones and devices are made for adults.'[1]

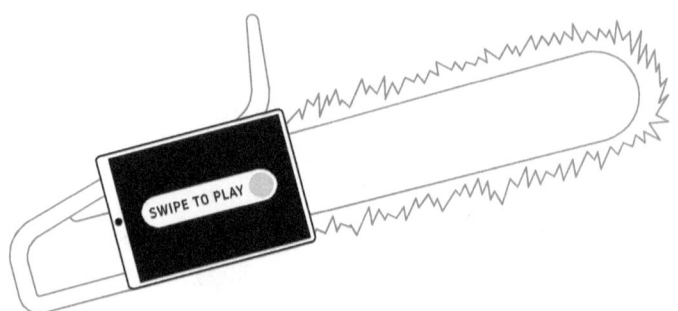

---

* While the emphasis of this chapter is on smartphones, many of the principles are also true for tablets and laptops.

Think about how I set up my son with the chainsaw – using a phone safely involves similar principles. Both are powerful tools and both require adequate preparation for safety and success. This involves discussions about the dangers and risks. It involves protective gear to guard your child against the worst elements of the internet. It requires that you show your child how and when to use the brake. And over time, keeping an eye on how they are progressing, you can celebrate when things go well or step in when things get out of hand. The alternative is to close your eyes and hope for the best. Not a smart strategy.

Setting up a child with a phone is not a one-and-done event. Our role is to assess the mental and emotional maturity of our children and set up their devices accordingly. It's a dance we continue for years, giving more freedom, over time, as our children learn to manage greater amounts of digital power.

GRADE UP AS THEY GROW UP

Let's return to one of our founding principles: minimise interactive screen media when children are young and grade up as they grow up.

If your child really needs a phone (for example, to call if they need you urgently), they don't necessarily need a *smartphone*. Flip phones are readily (and inexpensively) available to purchase online. When the time is right for you to buy your child a smartphone, dumb it down, at least to begin with. This means filtering online content and restricting some apps to reduce distraction. Think of it a bit like a probation period. Have lots of conversations with them about how to use the phone appropriately. Encourage healthier digital habits, then grade up as they grow up.

Here are four specific areas to consider when setting up your pre-teen or teen with a smartphone:

- device ownership
- digital contracts
- internet filters
- parental controls.

Let's have a look at each of these.

DEVICE OWNERSHIP

Managing money is important. We need to teach children the value of money and show them how to save for what they want. Except when it comes to buying a phone or other internet-enabled devices. It's better for parents to pay for and own their child's phone. It's about leverage.

From the beginning, my children knew that having a phone was a privilege and not a right. We own their devices and can take them back if needed. We have never had to do this, but there is leverage if a circuit-breaker is required in the future. The alternative is to encourage or allow children to save up for their own devices, and pay for their own data. It can work, but you lose a bit of power.

If they own the device, it's also harder to explain why you get to control their passwords, monitor their apps and shape how the device is used.

If your child has already saved for and purchased their own device, it's not too late. You can still recalibrate expectations. Let them know you have done some thinking and want to talk about adjusting how their device is set up and used. You may even choose to buy their phone from them to signal a shift in expectations. If your child is savvy they'll charge you full price!

DIGITAL CONTRACTS

A digital contract is a written agreement parents and children sign together, ideally before the child starts using a new phone. Like a memorandum of understanding, contracts create clarity and get everyone on the same page about expectations. This is not punitive but proactive. Renewed each year, parents and children get to talk about their mutual responsibilities and how they will succeed together – discussing expectations, setting healthy routines and pre-loading consequences should things go wrong.*

INTERNET FILTERS

No one likes to talk about the dark side of the web, including sex trafficking, online grooming and hard-core pornography. But we must be aware of these issues – 27% of all video content on the internet is pornographic or explicit in some way. To put this in perspective, in 2019 porn sites received more traffic than Amazon, Twitter and Netflix combined.[2] This is not a small issue. The average age of first exposure to pornography is 11 years old, and by 17 years old, nearly 50% of young men are regularly streaming violent, racist and misogynistic porn.[3] This is contributing to widespread mental health problems and relationship breakdowns in young people, and the perpetuation of violence against women.[4] In the words of Chris McKenna:

---

* To download an editable digital contract for phones, tablets and laptops, please visit www.raisinghumans.au/parenting-resources.

when it comes to online pornography, 'it is time for every parent on earth to leave the ignorance of the land of *if*, and embrace the reality of *when*.'[5]

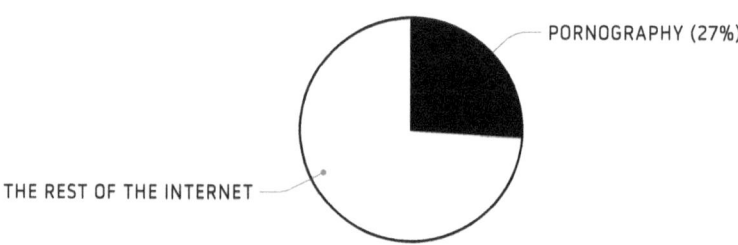

By downloading and installing filtering software, you can block access to adult websites and other unwanted internet activity at home. Internet filters are no silver bullet, of course, but they do provide frontline protection against the worst elements of the web. This is an ever-changing landscape, but at the writing of this book there are two common ways to filter your home internet. The first is to install internet filtering software on individual devices. The second is to install a filter at a Wi-Fi level, so that any device using your home Wi-Fi signal is protected.

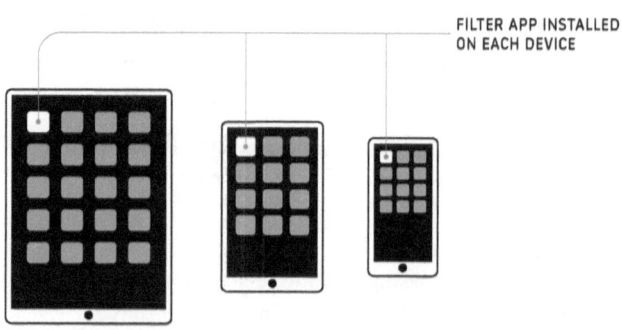

AGE-APPROPRIATE SETUP | 63

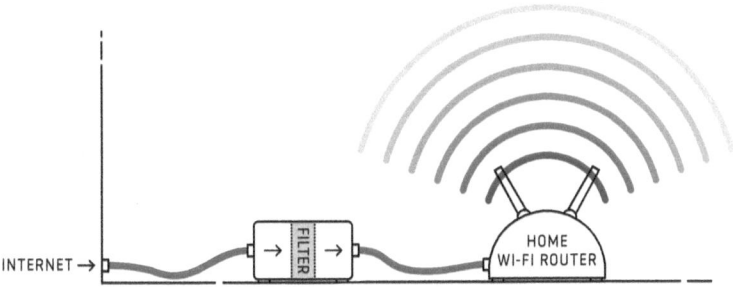

ALL HOME WI-FI INTERNET ACCESS IS FILTERED

There are advantages and disadvantages to these approaches, and both have their challenges. Most internet filtering companies provide advice and support to help parents set up the software at home.*

PARENTAL CONTROLS

Parental controls are features within the operating system of your child's phone (for example, Apple iOS or Android OS) that allow you to manage and restrict what they can do on that device. These features are easy to set up and quite effective, and provide basic protection (even without third-party internet filtering software). Features differ from system to system, but common controls include:

- **Screen-time limits** to disable specific apps and phone functions at set times of the day, or after a certain amount of usage. For example, you can block the internet after 8:30pm on weeknights, or restrict social media usage to 30 minutes a day.

---

* I have included links to a number of internet filtering companies on my website – please visit www.raisinghumans.au/parenting-resources.

- **Communication limits** to restrict making or receiving phone calls or text messages at set times; for example, during school hours.
- **Content and privacy restrictions** to block particular apps or groups of apps (for example, games or social media). You can also restrict the streaming of adult-rated content from certain websites.
- **Ask to buy features** to block or restrict in-app purchases to ensure your child asks for permission before installing or deleting apps. This is also a safeguard against racking up debt through expensive in-app purchases.

All of these settings require a parental passcode. Select a passcode that your children can't guess and keep it secret.

When setting up our daughter with her first phone, we used parental controls to make her smartphone less powerful; that is, no games, no social media and limited times when she could use the internet. As she gets older, demonstrating healthy routines, self-awareness and self-control, we'll increase her freedoms. It's about an ongoing conversation with give and take, keeping our relationship at the front of our mind as we make decisions.

To find out more about how to set up parental controls of your child's specific phone, search online for 'parental controls for [type of phone]'.

A NOTE ABOUT SOCIAL MEDIA AND GIRLS

Jonathan Haidt, one of the world's leading experts in moral psychology, is outspoken about the dangers of social media for teenage girls, particularly in middle school.

Social media is increasingly linked with mental health issues, and girls are more susceptible than boys: 'Girls who use social media heavily are about two or three times more likely to say that they are depressed than girls who use it lightly or not at all.[6] Haidt argues there is enough evidence for us to 'start treating social media a bit like smoking or drinking,'[7] by increasing the age of minimum use and mandating mental health warnings when signing in. Because this is a social contagion issue, schools also need to get involved, with principals setting a norm of no social media until high school. Parents must actively discourage social media with their girls until at least 14, or ideally 16, years of age.

If you are a parent with a young girl, it seems wise to follow Haidt's suggestions. Say 'no' to all social media until at least high school, including Instagram, Snapchat, TikTok and others. While platforms differ, all social media seems to be harmful to young girls. These services heighten self-consciousness and amplify insecurities. They enable relational bullying as girls jostle to find out where they fit in the social pecking order. The algorithms on these platforms purposefully emphasise body image, and 'likes' and 'hearts' amplify social anxiety.*

ONE SMALL STEP

At this point, I imagine you may be feeling overwhelmed by the complexity of setting up an age-appropriate phone. I feel your pain. I wish there was an easier way. But momentum starts with a single step. Listed below are specific ideas to consider. Select one task and take action!

---

* One of the reasons parents give their children social media is because they worry their children will be socially isolated from their friends. But research indicates the opposite – young people who spend *more* time on social media report feeling *more* lonely and left out.

Device ownership:

- [ ] Can you save $30 a week towards your child's first phone?
- [ ] Can you drip feed information to your child to build the expectation that when they get a phone, there will be restrictions?
- [ ] If your child already has a phone, can you start a conversation with your pre-teen to develop better boundaries? 'I think we made a mistake giving you a phone without enough safeguards. Can we talk about some changes … '

Digital contracts:

- [ ] Can you download and read the example contracts on my website?
- [ ] Can you talk with your child about the need to sign a digital contract in the future?
- [ ] Can you ask how your child is feeling about their phone habits, to warm them up for a future conversation about better boundaries?

Internet filters:

- [ ] Can you follow the link to my website and spend half an hour reviewing different software options?
- [ ] Can you ask your friends if they use internet filters and how well they work?
- [ ] Can you have an honest conversation with your spouse or partner about the risks of pornography exposure and how you might start a conversation with your son or daughter?

Parental controls:

- ☐ Can you watch a five-minute video about how parental controls work for your child's model of phone?
- ☐ Can you read more information about the harms of social media on young people, particularly teenage girls?
- ☐ Can you watch a documentary like *The Social Dilemma* with your kids and talk about their experiences with social media?

IN SUM

- Phones are powerful tools and must be handed over with safety. Remember the story about my son using a chainsaw.

- When your child receives their first smartphone, dumb it down. Restrict apps and filter the internet to ensure they get off to a healthy start. Then grade up as they grow up.

- Digital contracts are essential to communicate expectations and establish boundaries from the beginning. You can re-sign every year and continue the conversations.

- Internet filters are programs to block the worst of the internet. Remember that online pornography is grabbing our boys by the eyeballs and we need to do something about this.

- We need to be informed about the negative impacts of social media on mental health, particularly for young girls. Let's say 'no' to all social media until at least high school.

- Parental controls are in-built functions to manage and restrict what your child can do on that device. Set a password and keep it safe. Use these controls until your child is old enough to demonstrate healthy levels of self-care and self-restraint.

> **SOMETHING TO THINK ABOUT**
>
> Do you think of a smartphone as a powerful tool? How does this impact the way you go about setting it up for your children?

CHAPTER 7

REGULAR TALK

1 THESSALONIANS 5: 11 'Encourage one another and build each other up, just as in fact you are doing.'

You do not have to be an expert to talk. That's good news, because talking regularly with your kids is one of the most important things you can do. Every child is different and every stage of their development brings challenges, but if we communicate regularly along the journey we will have given them a great start to life. Ongoing, open and judgement-free communication is essential to help a child navigate the online world.

If 'location, location, location' is the catchcry for retail owners then 'relationship, relationship, relationship' is wisdom for parenting.

Communication is a two-way exchange. This means listening not lecturing, asking questions and being engaged.* We can

---

* Many parents don't realise they are using an adult 'lecturing voice' when talking with their children. Try softening your tone using these sentence structures: 'I've been wondering about … ' and 'I've noticed … '.

strengthen our relationships with our children by discussing the media they are consuming. As challenging as technology can be, it's also one of the best ways we can engage in our children's world. We can mimic heroes and learn from villains. We can reinforce positive messages and challenge unhelpful narratives. So let's look for opportunities to talk regularly about technology with our children and do so in creative ways.

In this chapter we'll be exploring the importance of moulding our child's character through the conversations we have around digital media. This involves connection and critique within the broader context of healthy screen-time boundaries. So let's talk early and often in their younger years to establish a culture where our children feel safe to talk about anything.

POSITIVE AND SHARED ENGAGEMENT

Digital media is spectacular. There are many ways to enjoy the wonders of the online world as a family. You might watch a movie together or talk about your favourite shows. Or kick back on the couch and listen to each other's music. Or become avatars with assault rifles and blow each other to pieces – a counterintuitive way to bond as a family! There are so many ways to enjoy media with our children if we are willing to enter their world and participate in what they are interested in.

We made a decision early on to watch shows with our young children, learning the names of various characters and discussing what we thought about their behaviours. As our kids moved into primary school, we encouraged them to watch television together, side by side on the couch rather than using individual devices. This worked well in the younger years when our kids were watching G and PG movies. It became more difficult in lockdown when they needed their own laptops for online learning. It stopped working as they approached their teens and became interested in different shows. Even still, our children are only allowed to use their laptops to watch TV in the lounge room, rather than in separate places around the house. This is about encouraging everyday conversations and reinforcing our family value of togetherness.

Another strategy to engage positively with media is to start a family movie night. A weekly movie can be a great way to connect and talk about various topics as a family. For a season, we watched animated movies. Then documentaries. Then cult classics with worthwhile content. And of course, no movie is complete without ice-cream. If you need help selecting suitable movies for your family, there are plenty of ideas online. We refer to Common Sense Media, a website that shares information about the suitability of digital content for children.* We don't always agree with their recommendations, but it can be a useful

---

* https://www.commonsensemedia.org.

starting place to get a sense of the age-appropriateness of a movie or program.

One of the reasons we talk about media with our children is to stay engaged in what they are interested in. This can be hard, and increasingly so, when your children hear about violent movies or video games that 'everyone is watching' at school and feel they're missing out. This is difficult, particularly when some popular shows or games are clearly age inappropriate. Positive engagement does not mean 'going with the flow' to the detriment of your child's mental, emotional and spiritual health. Sometimes parents just have to be brave enough to have the conversation: 'I'm sorry this is hard, but we do things differently in our family. We love you too much to let you watch things that are bad for your brain. But let's have a think about what we *can* say "yes" to instead!'

There was a time when my youngest son became interested in video games. He loves competition and all his friends were gaming, but he wasn't great at regulating his emotions after playing these games. My son also likes chess and has a knack for strategic thinking, so we tried to find an alternative that might pique his interest. We discovered Civilisation VI, a turn-based strategic game that's engaging without the flashing colours, social cues or intermittent reward loops embedded in newer console games. It was a hit! My son gets to build cities, create trade partnerships and pillage gold. For better or worse, I have also become engrossed in this game, giving my son and me something to talk about. We debate the best ways to advance scientific achievements. We discuss tactics to overcome barbarian encampments. We talk through the morality of using nuclear weaponry to overcome enemy strongholds. My son is now more advanced at this game than I am, teaching me new strategies.

Similarly, my wife has done a fantastic job at staying connected with my teenage daughter by watching dramas together. They have a girls' night each week and talk about whatever comes up (including the 'eye candy'). This is good for their relationship and it's good for me – I will never have to watch *Gilmore Girls*.

None of this is rocket science. Connect positively using media. Find out what your children are interested in. Watch what they watch. Talk about it. With a bit of creativity we can engage positively with digital media in our children's lives, staying connected and helping them learn, without capitulating to everything others are doing.

CONSTRUCTIVE CRITIQUES

Like the curator of a museum, we are responsible for overseeing the types of art our children consume online. Remember, the role of a parent is to raise an adult. We want our children to become healthy, contributing members of society with character traits such as patience, kindness, goodness and self-control. Unfortunately, the entertainment industry has a different vision. Many of the teenagers seen on television are moody, selfish and impulsive. They are obsessed with physical beauty. They sleep around. They seek revenge. They reject the wisdom of elders. They buy consumer goods and, of course, adore their devices. I struggle with this archetype and want to pass on a healthier vision of life for my children as they grow up. This is why we teach them to critique the media they consume.

From an early age, we have tried to instil in our children a healthy scepticism of the messages hidden within popular culture. We started with the 'advert game', pausing during a show to discuss the commercials.[1] I would ask, 'What did this company just promise you?' After some thought, my young kids would give their responses: 'Drinking Coke makes you happy?', 'Drinking Coke gives you friends?', 'Drinking Coke makes you pretty?' 'Spot on,' I'd say, 'But it's not true. Let's keep watching.' Nowadays the advert game has become more sophisticated as the ads we watch are the movies themselves. So we talk about the stories within the story. 'What did this movie just promise you?' ... 'Love is a feeling and not a commitment.' 'Having sex with strangers has no consequence on your future marriage.' 'Hating your parents is how you discover your true self.' 'Spot on,' I'd say, 'But it's not true. Let's keep watching.'

RELATIONSHIP, RELATIONSHIP, RELATIONSHIP

Equipping our children for the world they inhabit has always been an important part of parenting. Media is such a significant part of our children's lives and creates myriad opportunities to talk. Isn't Harry Potter brave? I wonder if Anakin's decision to revenge his mother impacted his heart? Did we actually wear clothes like the kids on *Stranger Things*? So many rich conversations!

Be curious and engage in what your children are interested in. Try to relate, not react. At the same time, help them critique the messages hidden within the stories they watch, and curate content in age-appropriate ways. If you can create a culture where your kids feel safe to talk with you about anything, you're well and truly on your way to withstanding the tougher years. For conversations create culture, supported by patterns and rhythms – the focus of our next chapter.

IN SUM

- Parenting is about 'relationship, relationship, relationship'. We can build and maintain relationships with our children by talking about their media interests.

- Take time to watch movies and play video games with your children to positively engage in their world. This can be enjoyable, help you stay connected and keep you up to date with the characters shaping their world views.

- Talk about the media you watch with your children, sharing your values and perspectives along the way. Family movie night can be a fun way to connect and talk with your children about meaningful things.

- Like the curator of a museum, parents are responsible for overseeing the types of media their children consume. Teach your kids to critique the messages hidden within popular media, shaping their perspectives in line with your family values.

SOMETHING TO THINK ABOUT

Do you find it easier to affirm and connect with your children using media, or to challenge and critique what they are viewing? How might you calibrate positive affirmation and constructive critique in a healthy, balanced way?

CHAPTER 8

TECH-HEALTHY RHYTHMS

1 TIMOTHY 4:7-8 'Train yourself to be godly. For physical training is of some value, but godliness has value for all things, holding promise for both the present life and the life to come.'

Families function best when they orientate their activities around routines and rhythms. For example, newborn babies benefit from consistent sleep, feed and play routines. Children also do better with consistency. As much as children may complain about cleaning their teeth or practising the piano, the routines and rhythms of family life help them learn and grow. By rhythms, I mean the habitual patterns and behaviours we train our children to do over time. The predictability of these patterns helps children feel safe and communicates what matters to us as a family.

RHYTHMS COMMUNICATE VALUES AND CREATE CULTURE

As part of the STARTER Framework we have spent time discussing how to shape a child's environment by eliminating access to certain devices. According to habit expert James Clear, external controls are an effective way to guide behaviour: 'It is not necessary to change a person in order to change their behaviour. Just change their environment.'[1] By adding or removing barriers to digital use, we can effectively influence how our children spend their digital time when they are young.

Externally imposed guardrails such as filters and parental controls are effective to a point, then they stop working because external limits work on behaviour and not the heart. As children grow up, they need to learn to manage their own digital environments, exhibiting self-awareness and self-control. Filters and restrictions, while important, cannot train the human heart to desire what is healthy and wholesome. Children need digital boundaries but not in isolation – they also need training in how to make good decisions for themselves. This is where rhythms and patterns come in.

Tech-healthy rhythms are about culture setting as a family. The first step, as always, is to start with self – reviewing our own digital behaviours. The patterns we set as a family will inevitably become our family culture. Let's say, for example, you want your kids to be present and engaged at the dinner table. Start by silencing your own phone, leaving it unanswered when eating together. Talk about the importance of eating without interruption and the value you place on connecting each night as a family. Reinforce the behaviours you want to embed over time. Eventually, when your children get their own devices, the path is well worn. No screens during dinner is 'the way we do things around here'.[2]

Model. Talk. Embed.

Years later, when your teens become adults and start making their own decisions, it is likely they will embody the same values in their own households. There are no guarantees, of course, but the establishment of predictable patterns in line with our values guides our children towards adopting similar world views and behaviours. This is the power of predictable patterns. It is also why the STARTER Framework requires we start with self. The digital habits we model are the ones our children will mimic over time.

TECH-FREE RHYTHMS

Andy Crouch, author of *The Tech-Wise Family*, proposes that families disconnect from their devices 'one hour a day, one day a week, and one week a year'.[3] I like this pattern because it's clear and specific (if not aspirational). It's a great example of what it might look like to develop tech-healthy rhythms as a household.

For the remainder of this chapter, I will outline three high-value tech-healthy rhythms you might consider adopting as a family. My intention is to keep this short and practical rather than repeat research that is in my previous book.*

Here are three practical ideas to make a start:

- tech-free sleep
- tech-free meals
- tech-free car trips.

---

* In my previous book, *Spacemaker*, I outlined a series of annual, weekly and daily habits to make space for deep thought, deep rest and deep relationships away from a screen. Rather than rehash my previous work, I suggest you pick up a copy if you are interested in developing tech-healthy rhythms for yourself and your family.

TECH-FREE SLEEP

Phones and sleep do not mix. According to research:

- One in three teens say they are on their phones at night when their parents think they are asleep[4]
- 10% of teens check their phone notifications more than 10 times a night[5]
- 73% of teens get insufficient sleep to function in an optimal way.[6]

Sleep is crucial for the overall health and wellbeing of young people. A lack of sleep impacts mental health, including focus and learning, and physical health, including appetite, metabolism, and immune, hormonal and cardiovascular functioning.[7] If you want to establish healthy tech-free rhythms as a family, start by reclaiming the bedroom for sleep.

When I speak to parents around the country, most end their day by scrolling on their phones in bed. One partner plays Candy Crush while the other checks Instagram. Then, in the morning, we reach for our phone, which is also our alarm clock, and habitually open email, or social media, or the news – whatever app appeals to our identity. Rather than beginning the day with silent contemplation, we're filling our minds with other people's thoughts, other people's worries, and other people's bad news, setting the scene for a digitally distracted day. It's not good for us and it's not good for our children.

The solution is to make bedrooms a phone-free zone for parents and children alike. Shape the path by purchasing a charging dock with multiple ports and placing it in a shared living space. Set screen-time limits to disconnect all phones at night – let's say 8:00pm for tweens and 9:30pm for teens and parents – teaching your family to bookend each day with a bit of space. By creating a rhythm where every bedroom is a screen-free zone you will encourage a better night's sleep.

Having spoken with thousands of parents around the country, the biggest barrier to bookending our day with space is a practical one: how will we wake without our phone alarm? If this is an issue for you, here are some solutions:

- Can you buy an old-fashioned alarm clock?
- Can you use a vibrating sports tracker to wake you up instead?
- Can you use an old mobile phone that has no SIM card or access to the internet as an alarm clock?

Sleep is important. Create a tech-free bedtime and morning routine as a family. By training your children to sleep well you will set them up for life.

TECH-FREE MEALS

Eating a meal around a table is no longer a given. I was training a group of young professionals located in New York, to help them invest in deeper relationships as a remote team. After I explained the benefits of a tech-free meal, a lady in her mid-twenties raised her hand and commented: 'My flatmates and I have just started eating a meal together on a Wednesday night. We take turns cooking for each other and sit around a table. It's so fun!' The collective response was: 'Wow, we should try that. What a great idea. How funny ... you sound like you're living in the 1950s!' (This was the moment I officially realised I am middle-aged.) I didn't know how to respond. No one on the Zoom call had regularly eaten a family meal at the dining table when growing up, and the idea of eating without technology was so foreign that it conjured up images of the 'olden days'. This is a problem, because according to research, sharing a tech-free meal is one of the most important things we can do to communicate love and strengthen bonds as a family.

According to habit expert Charles Duhigg, 'Families who habitually eat dinner together raise children with better homework skills, higher grades, greater emotional control and more confidence.'[8] Eating together is also associated with better numeracy and literacy skills in younger children. So let's turn off our televisions and put away our devices. Reset, and make the dinner table a digital-free zone and create the simple habit of eating and talking together each day, without distraction.

TECH-FREE CAR TRIPS

In *The Tech-Wise Family*, Andy Crouch suggests that 'car time is conversation time'.[9] I have found this to be a helpful rule. In our family, some of the best conversations happen on the road. Our children will be looking out the window, talking about nothing in particular, and suddenly ask a meaningful question. Rather than one-syllable responses we end up with free-flowing conversation. This is possible because we have established a car trip norm that encourages social interaction.

When we gave our daughter noise-cancelling earbuds for Christmas, we set a few basic conditions. When we're together, like eating, playing board games or in the car, earbuds are to be put in their case. While our car time is not tech-free, we do choose to listen to the same music together. No individual devices. No earbuds. No earmuffs! Car time is conversation time, or at the very least a time to connect with each other. Sure, our kids may fight and argue because something isn't fair. Sometimes mum and dad have to live with hip-hop music. But our family car rhythm is important. It helps us communicate and negotiate. It is character forming and relationship bridging. It communicates the importance of togetherness, training our children to establish times when they turn on and turn off their technology.

FIND YOUR OWN RHYTHM

Every family is different and so the patterns you choose will be unique. We have developed rhythms around our five family values of: *fun, faith, physical activity, community* and *life-long learning*. As a result, we play board games and share jokes. We attend church and pray regularly as a family. We go outdoors and exercise. We eat a meal with friends every week. We carve out time to read and encourage deeper questions. Most of these activities are tech-free or at least tech-conscious. To find your own rhythm, think about the values and character traits you hope your children might embody and habituate these as predictable patterns. By setting healthy digital and non-digital rhythms as a family you can train and equip your children to think intentionally about the tech they use, why they are using it and when to live life unplugged.

IN SUM

- Families function best when they orientate their activities around routines and rhythms. Be thoughtful about the tech and non-tech rhythms you create as a family.

- Externally imposed guardrails such as filters and parental controls are effective to a point. Then they stop working. As our children grow up, they will need to adopt healthy tech rhythms for themselves.

- The patterns we establish communicate our family values and culture. Model, talk and embed certain norms until they become 'the way we do things around here'.

- Every family is different and therefore the patterns we adopt will be different. Three high-value rhythms to consider are tech-free sleep, tech-free meals and tech-free car trips.

SOMETHING TO THINK ABOUT

What is one family value you would like to pass on to your children? For example, kindness, generosity or hard work? Can you think of a predictable pattern that might help you communicate and embed this value as a family?

CHAPTER 9

ENCOURAGE ADVENTURES

MATTHEW 14:29 'Then Peter got down out of the boat, walked on the water and came toward Jesus.'

Young children are often fearless when it comes to heights, but I was sitting at the top of a gigantic slide 15 metres above the ground, palms sweating, eyes wide open and gripped by fear. It had taken me about five minutes to climb to the top of this tower and now, looking down, I wasn't sure if I had the guts to launch. My best friend had already made the plunge and survived. But here I was, feeling sick to the stomach, with a queue of people growing behind me. No chickening out now. Oh heck, here we go … argghhh!!

For most of us life was adventurous when we were young. There was risk and challenge, making life exhilarating. Take Monash for example, an adventure playground located in the Riverland of South Australia, my home state. Established in

1967 by a philanthropic entrepreneur, this playground featured more than 200 hand-made play pieces, and entry was free. By the mid 1980s, Monash was attracting 300,000 people a year.[1] As a family we came to enjoy the rides, including the giant metal slide that terrified me as a kid. The slide was so hot in summer that we sat on hessian bags to stop ourselves from burning. This playground was unbelievably fun. There were giant metal giraffes that rocked back and forth at a dizzying height, a flying fox (or zip line) with no safety harness, a number of spaceship-sized rotary cones, and a DIY roller coaster where we would sit in a metal box and hope not to die.

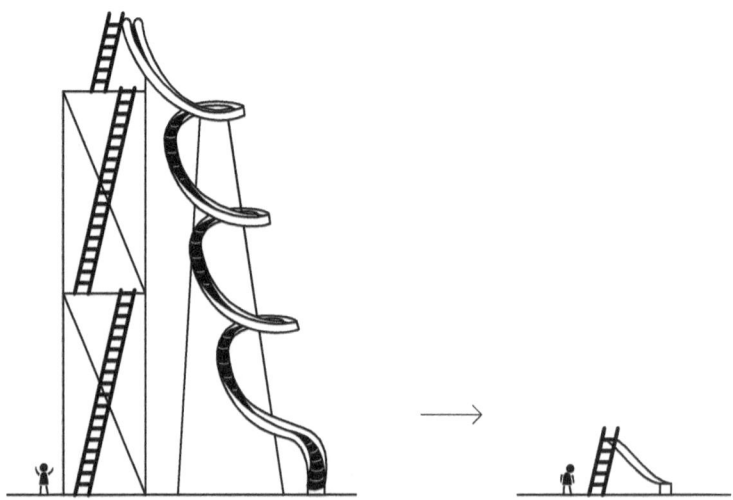

No doubt there were broken bones and plenty of scratches, but this was part of the excitement.

The original playground closed in 1992, after a visitor filed an insurance and injury claim against the council. A few years later, after lots of negotiation, Monash reopened as a child-safe park designed and run by the council. The 15-metre high metal slide was replaced by a safety-focused plastic tube about two metres from the ground. Giraffes were exchanged for ergonomic swings and rotary cones for a docile carousel. Even the ground was made safer, with rubber mulch replacing the original gravely soil. The new Monash playground is not bad by modern standards, but it's no longer life changing, character forming or memory making. Like many things in our society, the cult of safety has removed risk, danger and uncertainty, and the cost is a loss of adventure.

I'm not saying we should ignore risk management or put our children in harm's way. I wonder how I would feel watching my child climb the old Monash slide in the hot sun! But I do wonder if we have gone too far? Might our safety-obsessed culture be contributing to children being more anxious and less resilient than previous generations? When our children stay indoors, trading outdoor adventure for online gaming, is this really better for their wellbeing? Could our obsession with safety, unintentionally, be making them less safe?

KIDS ARE NOT FRAGILE BUT ANTIFRAGILE

According to bestselling authors Greg Lukianoff and Jonathan Haidt, we have created a culture where parents keep their children indoors and online under the guise of safety. But rather than protecting our children, helicopter parenting might be damaging their mental and emotional health, reducing their ability to thrive.[2]

If we look at the science of physical conditioning, the way to build muscle bulk is to extend our bodies, lifting heavy weights until we fatigue. When we do this, we stimulate micro-tears in our muscle fibres, activating a repair process that results in larger, stronger muscles.

The same is true when it comes to developing resilience in our children.

Children are not fragile, like teacups, but antifragile, like muscles. They need adventure and challenge to grow physically and mentally strong. In the words of Lukianoff and Haidt:

> Children, like many other complex adaptive systems, are antifragile. Their brains require a wide range of inputs from their environments in order to configure themselves for those environments. Like the immune system, children must be exposed to challenges and stressors (within limits, and in age-appropriate ways), or they will fail to mature into strong and capable adults, able to engage productively with people and ideas that challenge their beliefs and moral convictions.[3]

In other words, if we want to raise healthy, resilient tweens and teens we're going to need to encourage them to take risks, make mistakes, even hurt themselves from time to time.[4] We need to encourage adventures.

WHAT IS AN ADVENTURE?

Having an adventure does not mean you have to participate in dangerous activities like high-adrenalin sports (as fun as these can be). My use of the term 'adventure' is broad and inclusive, referring to any real-world activity that stretches our children to grow beyond their current capacity. When we throw a ball it requires strength and skill. When we learn to summersault on a trampoline there's a possibility we might get hurt. When we walk to the shops without supervision, there's a certain level of risk. The aim is to gradually and thoughtfully expand a child's ability to cope with stress and uncertainty by placing them in situations where they might struggle to perform, and therefore build resilience.

But having an 'adventure' online is not the same as having one in real life. Dying and regenerating on a computer game is not the same as falling on gravel and getting up. In the physical world there is no reset button. You get one chance to make the winning shot in a basketball final. You get one chance to apologise to a best friend after betraying their trust. You get one chance to make a good impression at your job interview. You get one chance to win that girl's affections. In each of these situations, it's important to show up prepared, with years of practice under your belt. We want our children to use their bodies, practise relationships and persevere in demanding situations so they are strong and skilful when it really counts.

CAN YOU FIND A GREATER *YES*?

It takes energy to encourage adventures. This energy can be hard to muster when we already feel tired and stretched as parents. But it doesn't work to say 'no' to screens without encouraging our children to find a greater 'yes'. For it can be boring being stuck inside without stimulation. I'm not saying we should spend every moment entertaining our kids, but we will need to help them come up with alternative options and teach them how to make their own fun.*

This is harder than it used to be. When I was a boy, we went outdoors because all the kids in the street were outdoors. Everyone was riding bikes and building cubby houses and playing sport. But culture has changed, making it harder to get our

---

* There is a list of 100 fun screen-free activities to do with your children in the appendix.

children outside. Too many parents are fearful about leaving their children unsupervised, and even when we do send our kids on play dates they end up indoors on a screen.

But with a bit of creativity we can encourage adventures outdoors. Write a list of interesting activities for when you need inspiration. Our list includes flying kites, riding bikes, playing chess, kicking the soccer ball, shooting a bow and arrow, playing instruments, reading books, doing puzzles, eating pancakes – and more. There are also activities that cost money, like going bowling, playing minigolf, and laser tag. These are for special occasions, like school holidays, if finances allow.

In addition, now that our oldest child is in her mid-teens, she has the freedom to visit friends and spend time in the city without our supervision. We taught her to catch a bus by herself a few years ago, and she has the confidence to walk to the city, or ride an Uber if we can't drop her somewhere. This has been a work in progress, establishing trust and relaxing boundaries over time, in line with her growing maturity.

Adventures can be positive and interesting. The next time you say 'no' to more screens, can you positively reframe the conversation and focus on a greater 'yes'? What can you do that is more enjoyable and adventurous than habitually using a screen? Get your children outdoors. Help them enjoy their bodies. Encourage them to spend time with their friends in creative ways.

SOMETIMES YOU JUST HAVE TO SAY *GO*

Last week, I made a proactive decision to take my children on an adventure. We live near the base of a mountain and I wanted to explore a walking track called 'The Lost World'. This track meanders down a gulley and ends at a series of caves and underground tunnels. Energised, my wife and I packed our day bags, made sandwiches and changed the batteries in our torches. The only thing our children had to do was put on their jackets and get in the car. This is when the challenge began.

My youngest son was adamant he would not be coming. He was enjoying a 'pyjama day' and wanted to continue playing his computer games. At first, my wife and I encouraged him, saying it would be lots of fun. When that didn't work, I tried to connect with him relationally, sitting beside him to engage in his game (before bringing up the walk one more time). Again, he refused. Then I put my foot down. I expressed in no uncertain terms that we were going on a family outing, together, and that if he refused to join us there would be no screens, including family movie night, for the rest of the holidays. This was a big threat and I was willing to follow through, even if it made life difficult for us all. My son reluctantly complied and stomped his way to the car.

Thankfully, we had an amazing time together. We talked and laughed as we neared the summit, including my youngest son. We trundled through mud and scrambled over craggy rocks together. The kids were excited to discover we needed to abseil down a rope to enter the heart of the cave, then squeeze through a tiny gap between two rocks, surrounded by complete darkness. When we emerged, we knew we had accomplished something special. We sat on a rocky outcrop overlooking our city and drank hot chocolate in thankfulness.

Five days after caving on the mountain, we asked our children to share the highlight of their week. When it came to my youngest son responding, can you guess what he shared? That's right – his most magical moment of the week was our adventure to The Lost World. He loved the darkness of the cave. He loved the challenge of scaling a rope. He loved tramping through mud together. Thank goodness for tough love parenting. Thank goodness for adventures.

IN SUM

- Children are not fragile, like teacups, but antifragile, like muscles. They need challenge, risk and adventure to grow physically and mentally strong.

- An adventure can be any real-world activity that stretches a child to grow beyond their current capacity. It's important to send our children outdoors.

- Unlike a computer game, there are no reset buttons in real life. An online 'adventure' does not build a child's resilience in the same way as falling down and getting up in the physical world.

- When we say 'no' to more screen time, it's important to help our children discover a greater 'yes'. Can you help them think about positive, life-giving alternatives? Brainstorm a list of interesting activities to do together and tackle these over time.

- Sometimes as parents we just have to say 'go'. Are you willing to take your children on adventures even if they don't want to go?

SOMETHING TO THINK ABOUT

Take a moment to reflect on some of your best childhood memories. Did they involve adventures? Were they outdoors? How might you replicate similar experiences with your own family?

CHAPTER 10

RELY ON OTHERS

ACTS 2:44 'All the believers were together and had everything in common.'

Parenting is personal. Really personal.

When I started working as a church minister many years ago, someone warned me I needed to tread carefully when speaking about certain things. They mentioned two areas of life in particular where people are sensitive and overly defensive. One is the way we use our money. The other is how we parent.

At the time I didn't have kids and this made no sense at all. Why would parents get defensive about hearing sound advice from others? Why would they not welcome input – even from other parents – to help them avoid foreseeable mistakes?

But now I'm a parent, I get it. We pour our heart and soul into our children and, despite our best efforts, feel inadequate at every stage. The upstairs brain can understand the logic of receiving loving critique – 'hey, I notice you tend to give in to your children when they nag' – but the downstairs brain shuts down the conversation. It's too painful and too personal. So we justify and defend, rationalising our emotions to avoid input from others. 'You don't know what my child is like ... your kid is no angel either ... at least I'm not uptight and inflexible!'

Even still, it's worth resisting the urge to bunker down and pretend things are fine when they're not. Parenting in a community is better than parenting alone. There is tremendous value in walking the journey with others as we seek to raise tech-healthy humans.

THE POWER OF VULNERABILITY

The late M. Scott Peck once suggested that 'there can be no vulnerability without risk; and there can be no community without vulnerability; and there can be no peace – ultimately no life – without community.'[1] I have come to agree with him. But it's hard to be vulnerable. It's hard to let people in. It's hard to let friends and family give us advice when we're sleep deprived and struggling with doubt, frustration and exhaustion. But if we become brave enough to share our parenting fears and open our hearts and minds to the input of others, the results are beneficial for everyone. We learn. We grow. We become like family. This is why vulnerability leads to community – it's an antidote to the otherwise lonely journey of parenting.

What does vulnerability look like in practice? According to Brené Brown, it's the courage to show up and let yourself be seen.[2] This means giving and receiving; the willingness to pour out and allow others to pour back in. For to accept help is often harder than to give help. It takes courage to reach out to friends for support when we are sick and struggling. It takes humility to receive a meal when we've had a bad week. It takes guts to admit when our parenting strategies have stopped working, and more courage still to listen to alternatives. This type of vulnerability is rare in our culture and hard to learn. But if we can approach our relationships with more vulnerability, allowing ourselves to be seen as we really are, we provide a gift to our children, our communities and our world.

IN SEARCH OF A DIGITAL COUNTER-CULTURE

I was talking with a client who was implementing the practices in my last book to make a bit more space in her life. Belinda had made personal gains but was struggling to help her children as well: 'Unplugging is really hard for our kids. My husband and I made a choice not to buy tablets but the other day my son came home, so excited, because one of his friends has an iPad. They play it together on the bus. Now instead of looking out the window, my son spends every morning and every afternoon playing on his friend's device. What can you do? The culture is stacked against us!'

This conversation is challenging because we can't control the society our children are growing up in. For better and worse, they are surrounded by a digital culture that promises technology as the path to freedom and self-expression. We can swim against the tide but it takes effort. While there are no easy answers, here's what I do know for certain. It is easier to parent in a community and harder to parent alone. This is why the STARTER Framework encourages us to rely on others. There is tremendous value in forming counter-cultural communities around our children, with people we know and trust. It's far easier to raise tech-healthy children when our friends are also being intentional in the way they introduce electronic media in their households.

IT TAKES A VILLAGE

We all know 'it takes a village to raise a child'. But how might you start if you don't have a village?

There are many ways to discover groups of likeminded people. You might connect with a mothers' group, or school association, or parenting program. You might meet people in your workplace that you gel with. Or through a sports association. Or a book club. Or a church community. Or a medieval society. People are everywhere. Think about parents in your world who you would like to spend more time with – and who might be interested in sharing real conversations about parenting with you.

Next comes the hardest part – arranging your calendars to invest in each other's lives on a regular basis.

In the Western world, we are robustly independent and believe our time is our own. As such, our lives have become so independent that many of us are finding it difficult to sync our schedules with other people, even our own families. But community needs regularity. We need predictable patterns to sustain relationships over time. And this may require that we surrender our personal autonomy for the good of the collective. That is, to turn up to a quiz night every Wednesday, even if we feel tired. Or to commit to a monthly coffee with friends. Or to remain loyal to a specific group of people, year after year, even when they can be emotionally draining.

MONDAY	TUESDAY	WEDNESDAY	THURSDAY	FRIDAY	SATURDAY	SUNDAY
		NOT MY TIME				NOT MY TIME
		NOT MY TIME				NOT MY TIME

Before my wife and I had children, we used to head to the pub every Sunday at 6pm. A group of friends from our church met at the same pub every week, and we made it a priority to turn up. Over time, lots of different people entered this pattern. Friends from different facets of our lives – work, sport, friends of friends – all realised they could find us at the pub at 6pm, resulting in a steady flow of people engaging in our world. Interestingly, I don't like pubs and I don't particularly enjoy drinking alcohol. But this is where our community wanted to be and so we made this commitment ahead of our personal preferences.

Things changed after our first child was born. We continued the pub pattern for about six months, baby in a basinet under the table, but soon realised this wasn't sustainable. Meeting at a pub wasn't going to help us build a community of young families for our current season of life. So we started to think creatively about how to find a new pattern. Other people in our friendship group had young children, so we began meeting in parks, then at the beach, eventually landing with a meal in our houses. I love that our children have grown up eating with people on a regular basis. In my mind, hospitality is a timeless and effective way to build an authentic community (in our case, oriented around food, faith and friendship). We started with one family and now eat with many families – rotating the cooking and sharing a pot luck to lighten the load. And while eating a meal with friends is our longest-lasting rhythm, we have enjoyed different patterns in different seasons, including a monthly firepit in our backyard, board-game nights, and seasonal celebrations such as Christmas carols with neighbours.

Community takes effort but it doesn't have to be complicated. It begins with a commitment to enter each other's lives. Be intentional. Find likeminded people you enjoy (and want your children to be around). Be thoughtful, generous and kind. Create a predictable pattern for your season of life and stick with it long enough to become a habit. Make a commitment to surrender the autonomy of your time by turning up even when you don't feel like company. Be vulnerable enough to talk about real things.

I understand not everyone can, or would want to, live the way we do. It's not essential to invest in a community of people to be a great parent or to raise tech-healthy humans. But sharing life can help. A great deal. If you're a single parent, or don't consistently have someone co-parenting alongside you, it can be harder to share life with others. But not impossible. In fact, the drive to connect with people can be a fantastic motivator to invest in new relationships. Is it possible to find another single parent who is keen for community and share a simple meal together as families? Or find a likeminded friend to debrief with when things get tough? Or share a family movie night with other families or friends? The opportunities are endless if you're willing to look.

IN SUM

- Parenting in a community is better than parenting alone. There is tremendous value in walking the journey with others as we seek to raise tech-healthy humans.

- Parenting is personal. It can be hard to let down our guard and rely on others, but a certain amount of vulnerability is needed to share life in a deep way.

- Parenting is never done in isolation but is influenced by broader societal trends. There is value in forming communities of likeminded parents who share similar parenting philosophies and tech beliefs.

- Community takes effort but it doesn't have to be complicated. It begins with a commitment to enter each other's lives by turning up, even when we don't feel like it.

SOMETHING TO THINK ABOUT

What are some of the practical benefits of parenting within a wider community of friends and family? What might this cost you? Is it worth the effort?

Below are three questions to help you stop, reflect and gain the most from what you have explored.

What *three significant insights* have arisen from what you have read so far?

What *two practical actions* will you commit to doing soon?

What *one big question* do you still have?

PART III
THE PATH FORWARD

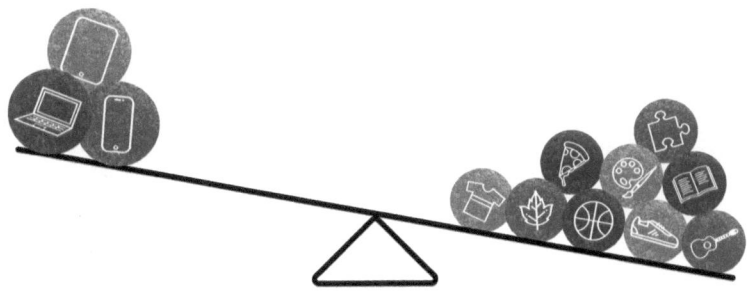

As a productivity consultant, I'm passionate about helping people take the next step. The best way to build momentum is to break goals down into small, manageable next steps and progress one task at a time. It really is as simple and as difficult as that.

You have already taken time out of your busy schedule to read this book. For this I am grateful. But now, as we reach the conclusion of this book, there are choices you need to make. In my thinking, you have three options.

The first is to skim over this part, read the last few pages and pat yourself on the back for having learnt something new. Not bad.

The second is to finish the book and spend time reflecting on what you have learnt, in the hope that you might apply something at an undetermined time in the future. A bit better.

The third, which I recommend, is to choose one small step *right now*, committing to tangible action in the next few days. This is possible even if you need more time to reflect on the content as a whole. According to research, momentum only builds when we take action – one step at a time, until we experience breakthrough.[1]

To help you make progress, I have developed a list of potential actions for each part of the STARTER Framework. This is not an exhaustive list but it will get you moving. Read this checklist with a pen or pencil in your hand. Write down one or two actions to complete in the next week. Consider how much time you will need for each action and block out time in your calendar to get started. Reward yourself and repeat the process.

If you get stuck or need further resources, please sign up and download the free parenting videos, checklists and infographic associated with this book: www.raisinghumans.au/faith.

I am also available if you want to work with me in person or online. My passion is to help busy people make space to think, rest, plan and breathe – and there are many ways to do this. I work with time-poor leaders and their teams to help them make space by becoming more productive. I speak at conferences to inspire audiences to make space by rethinking their relationship with the online world. I speak with parents to help them make space in their children's lives by establishing better digital and non-digital habits. I also work with school principals and teachers who want to make space for deeper conversations about the digital culture of their communities. If you are interested in engaging me to speak, train or work with your team, please visit my website (www.spacemakers.com.au) to email me or book a 15-minute Zoom conversation.

A link to my website is also available by scanning the QR code on the back pages of this book.

Now for a decision about what you will do next.

CHAPTER 11

THE STARTER FRAMEWORK CHECKLIST

Read this checklist and identify activities you would like to apply in your own context. Prioritise one or two actions and make a plan to get started as soon as possible.

Start with self:

- ☐ Disconnect from all devices for a 24-hour period and pay attention to how you feel. This is a heart check to help you reflect on your relationship with technology.
- ☐ Do a digital audit, a bit like keeping a food diary, where you write down everything you do for one week. For example, when do you first reach for your phone? What apps do you habitually use? How often do you check emails? The aim is to understand your digital habits and assess what you need to change.
- ☐ Get more information by reading my book *Spacemaker: How to unplug, unwind and think clearly in the digital age* to help you shift your digital paradigms and personal habits.

Take it slowly:

- ☐ Practise saying 'no' or 'not yet' to your child for small things, like eating dessert or watching television, and sticking with your decision when they complain or nag. Try offering a tangible timeline if you can: 'Not yet, but we can do this in 15 minutes/one hour/after lunch.'
- ☐ Spend time journalling your memories about your own childhood and the absence or presence of boundaries. Were your parents overly strict or overly flexible? How do your childhood experiences impact your parenting today – including things you want to repeat, and things you want to change?
- ☐ Write a pros and cons list to help you decide when to get your child a smartphone, considering the benefits and challenges in advance.

Age-appropriate setup:

- ☐ Choose a 'dumb' phone (no internet) instead of a smartphone to stay in contact with your kids when they are away from home.
- ☐ Download a digital contract and make a time to discuss it with your pre-teen or teen.
- ☐ Set up parental controls on your child's devices to reduce the risk of them engaging in adult content or unhealthy screen behaviours.

Regular talk:

- ☐ Reflect on your approach to engaging in technology with your children. Draw a line with a scale of 1 to 10,

with 1 being extremely negative and 10 being extremely positive. How negatively or positively do you view the role of technology in your children's lives? What about your partner? Is there a difference in your approaches and if so, how might you get on the same page?
- ☐ Observe what games and programs your children are most interested in and ask positive, non-judgemental questions to engage them conversationally.
- ☐ Watch a movie with your children and talk about the positive and negative messages in the story. This is an opportunity to hear what they think and contribute comments, where appropriate, guided by your own values.

Tech-free rhythms:

- ☐ Observe the tech and non-tech rhythms that exist in your family and reflect on what they say about your shared values.
- ☐ Eat a screen-free meal each day or night around a table.
- ☐ Buy a charging dock and charge your phone outside your bedroom, before talking with your children about doing the same.

Encourage adventures:

- ☐ Write a list of interesting activities to do as a family and start ticking them off one by one.
- ☐ Think about the personalities of your children and find a positive 'yes' to counteract the 'no' to more screens. For example, would your child enjoy a board game, or making a sandcastle, or baking a cake, or riding a bike,

or wrestling in the lounge room, or walking to the shops with their friends?
- [ ] Reflect on your parenting style and how you feel about exposing your children to risk and challenge (in an age-appropriate way). What might need to shift in your thinking to step back and encourage your children to roam?

Rely on others:

- [ ] Buy a copy of this book for a few friends and organise a time to discuss what you have learnt together. It could be the start of a parenting book club!
- [ ] Think of a friend you trust enough to share your struggles with in a vulnerable way. Is there anything stopping you from being honest with them?
- [ ] Think of anyone you might want to eat a simple meal with on a regular basis. Can you invite them over and see how it goes?

CONCLUSION

In preparing for this book, I asked my children to think about their best experiences in life. I loved their responses:

- 'I remember when you used to play the guitar to help us sleep. Sometimes you would read us the "star" book by shining a torch onto the ceiling. That was so much fun.'
- 'I remember when Dakota used to come around on the weekend and jump on the trampoline with us. That was so cool.'
- 'I remember playing minigolf as a family. Jethro was too young to join us and spent his time playing with a net, collecting golf balls from the surrounding water traps. At one point, he wandered in front of a moving ball. We all shouted, "Jethro, get out the way" and he ran, dragging the net behind him. The golf ball rolled right into his net and Jethro kept running. We said it was a hole in one and laughed so hard our stomachs hurt.'

On reflection, my children's best moments surprised me. Listening to a guitar in bed? Playing with a neighbour? Laughing at a golf ball in a net? These experiences might seem mundane and ordinary. Rather than costing a lot of money, they involved hanging out together and laughing with loved ones. They were tangible. They were relational. They were unplugged.

A WELL-LIVED LIFE

At the end of our time on earth when we reflect on the highs and lows of a life well lived, I suspect most of us will remember moments with loved ones immersed in real life.

If my children's reflections are anything to go by, our highs will be everyday ordinary experiences, like building sand castles on the beach, being hugged by a loved one, exploring nature or achieving meaningful goals with others. And similarly, having walked alongside people at the end of their life, I know that our hardest times – the terribly painful moments that shape us for better or worse – are also real and relational. We lament friendships lost, unresolved arguments, physical accidents, deaths and divorces. We regret risks we did not take. We regret time wasted on meaningless activities. We regret failing to cherish the important people in our lives.

We know this, intuitively. But it's hard to remember these realities when caught in the whirlwind of life. It's hard to keep an eye on the bigger picture when we're struggling to get by. This is where the STARTER Framework can be useful. It's a practical map to help us make tech-smart parenting decisions in the pre-teen years, one small step at a time.

We start by examining our own tech habits and behaviours. We encourage real-life experiences and relationships for the developing brain, taking it slowly when it comes to kids and interactive media. When the time is right, we use parental controls and digital contracts, establishing healthy tech and non-tech rhythms as a family. We talk about media, regularly, and how the messages in media connect with our values. And finally, rather than struggle alone, we do our best to parent with others, muddling along as a community to raise tech-healthy humans.

As challenging as tech-parenting may be, take heart! The most valuable parts of childhood remain the same. There is so much goodness for our children to experience in real life. I want my children to play imaginative games and go on treasure hunts. I want them to dress up as mermaids and slaughter dragons. I want them to stroll in nature and breathe fresh air, capturing memories without needing a photograph. I want them to wander along the beach in search of shells. And day dream. And laugh out loud. And wrestle with boredom. And learn to say sorry. And create their own fun when they have 'nothing to do'. In the mix, of course, I want my children to enjoy great movies, play video games, stream interesting music and connect with family and friends online. It's not about being tech-free but resetting to become tech-healthy, inspiring our kids to embrace the enormity of life, online and offline, with everything in its place.

ALL YOU NEED IS $30

When I speak with parents around the country, I hear some of their best parenting experiences. This is always fascinating. Like the stories shared by my children, the times we remember as parents are often relational, in person and otherwise ordinary. For example, one father told me about his best memory as a parent. Darryn works late most days but when he can, he catches the early train home to spend time with his son, throwing a rugby ball in the backyard for an hour. This means a lot to him. It also means the world to his son: 'My son loves throwing a ball with me. It's so simple really. And what does it cost? One ball. Maybe $30. That's all. But it's the highlight of my week. I know that one day, my son will look back and remember his time throwing a ball with his dad. It will probably be one of the highlights of his life. It certainly is mine.'

I love this. All we need is $30 and the willingness to throw a ball with our kids from time to time. Yes, it takes time, energy and intentionality, but these human interactions are incredibly important. Such events may seem ordinary and everyday, but at the end of our lives when we look back at what really mattered, it is these memories we will treasure the most. Almost anyone can throw a ball. Almost anyone can go for a walk. Almost anyone can disconnect from a screen for long enough to muck around with their kids in the rub of real life. Raising tech-healthy humans is as simple and as difficult as that.

APPENDIX

100 FUN NON-SCREEN ACTIVITIES TO DO WITH CHILDREN

1. Bike ride
2. Bush walk
3. Make fun things out of cardboard boxes
4. Write letters to friends or family
5. Make paper planes
6. Paint
7. Create a bouquet of wild flowers
8. Play sport (soccer, basketball, tennis, cricket, etc.)
9. Watch clouds and find 'cloud animals'
10. Make homemade fruit-juice icy poles
11. Shoot bow-and-arrows
12. Play mini-golf
13. Learn to whistle
14. Read books
15. Wash the car (with extra soap!)
16. Arm wrestle each other
17. Walk to the local shops to buy ice-cream
18. Practise skipping with a rope
19. Look for shells or rocks at the beach
20. Make cubby houses (inside or outside)
21. Plant trees
22. Blow bubbles
23. Go bowling

24. Bake a cake or brownies
25. Walk in the snow
26. Explore a cave
27. Go fishing
28. Fly a kite
29. Build Lego
30. Swim at the local pool
31. Play board games
32. Create a home disco with loud music and dancing
33. Enjoy bird watching
34. Make a Slip 'n' Slide with plastic and washing-up liquid
35. Play laser tag
36. Dress up in funny clothes
37. Do kitchen science experiments
38. Play cards
39. Have a scavenger hunt
40. Climb a tree (or build a tree house)
41. Play music or sing together
42. Hold a laughing contest (the first one to laugh loses)
43. Make mudpies
44. Fold origami
45. Listen to an album and talk about the lyrics
46. Build something out of trash
47. Draw on the pavement with chalk
48. Make pizzas (chocolate pizzas?)
49. Visit a library
50. Play in the park
51. Do a puzzle
52. Have an outdoor or indoor picnic
53. Exercise as a family
54. Go camping
55. Have a water balloon fight

56. Gaze at the stars at night
57. Eat an amazing brunch together
58. Create a huge line of dominoes and knock them over
59. Jump on a trampoline together
60. Throw and catch a ball
61. Skim stones
62. Feed the ducks, or seagulls, or pigeons at the park
63. Head out in the rain and splash in puddles
64. Learn to juggle
65. Create an obstacle course and time how long it takes to complete
66. Go roller-blading
67. Make lemonade
68. Learn to sew
69. Make sandcastles
70. Have messy fun (shaving foam, flour and water, glitter!)
71. Plant vegetables in the garden
72. Play charades
73. Host a mini-Olympics with a variety of creative events
74. Pick flowers and press them in wax paper
75. Make crazy hair styles with gel
76. Do a toy exchange with a friend
77. Paint your faces
78. Create a photo album or photo board
79. Wrestle each other
80. Create a time capsule
81. Practise and perform a play for your family or friends
82. Run through the sprinklers on a hot day
83. Have an outdoor fire and cook marshmallows
84. Walk your dog
85. Cook a meal for someone who is unwell
86. Build boats with sticks and leaves and race them in a river

87. Go to a skate park
88. Collect bugs
89. Play 'the floor is lava' with cushions
90. Learn and perform magic tricks
91. Have a teddy bear picnic or a tea party
92. Do weights together in a home gym
93. Make necklaces out of colourful pasta and dental floss
94. Set up a tent in the backyard and sleep out with friends
95. Write short stories and share them with each other
96. Paint your nails together
97. Visit a museum
98. Go to a café and drink hot chocolate
99. Bury a box and create a treasure map for others to find it
100. Housework and errands (yes, really – anything can be made fun when done together with a playful attitude!)

FREE ONLINE VIDEO SERIES

Struggling to raise kids in a screen-filled world?

I've created an online tech-parenting course to help you expand on the ideas in this book.

This free tech-parenting course includes:

- 15 high-quality videos
- Print-ready infographics
- Downloadable checklists
- Digital contracts... and more!

Sign up to receive this exclusive pack of bonus resources.

Visit www.raisinghumans.au/faith or scan the QR Code to get started.

ADDITIONAL PARENTING RESOURCES

In *Raising Tech-Healthy Humans*, I have suggested a number of resources, including digital contracts for phones, tablets and laptops. These are found on a reader-only page on my website, with downloadable resources and links to recommended books and videos.

By putting everything on a webpage (instead of inside this book), I can ensure resources stay up to date over time.

To access this private page, scan the QR code or visit: www.raisinghumans.au/parenting-resources.

ACKNOWLEDGEMENTS

There are three types of people in this world: smart people and dumb people.

My son told me this joke and I thought it was funny!

But seriously, writing a book is kind of a dumb thing to do. According to George Orwell, 'writing a book is a horrible, exhausting struggle, like a long bout of some painful illness. One would never undertake such a thing if one were not driven on by some demon whom one can neither resist or understand.' Writing my first book was agonising like in Orwell's description. I needed a sabbatical to recover. But this experience has been quite the opposite – both a joy and a delight – taking six weeks not six years to draft! This is largely because of the incredible team I have supporting me.

On the top of my thank-you list, as always, is my incredible wife, Kylie Sih, who for 20 years has been my companion and best friend. Not only is she an inspirational mother, but she is also a gifted editor and moulds the texture of what I write.

To my children, Naomi, Caleb and Jethro, thank you for allowing me to include our family stories in this book. You are a gift from God and a joy to so many people. I couldn't be a dad without you (dad joke!).

Thank you to my dear friends Michael, Julia, Aja, Mimi and Lexi, who have shared countless moments as my second family. It is a joy to share life, love and loss together. Life is richer because of you all.

Professionally, there are myriad people I want to thank. Mike Capuzzi – book coach extraordinaire – this book would not exist if I had not met you (even if my shook – short helpful book – morphed into a book). Thank you Michael Hanrahan, Anna Clemann, and the incredible publishing team at Publish Central for creating such a high-quality work. Thank you Kate Renshaw, Dr Rupa Wong, Belinda McLean, Kevin de Lacy, Leanne McLean, and other professionals who gave input to improve my manuscript. And thank you to everyone who works in and around the life of Spacemakers – Tim Hynes, Matt Bain, Elissa Lok, Tom Smith, Justin Mejos, Mark Kuilenberg, and others – you are deeply appreciated and make the work we do meaningful.

BUY *SPACEMAKER*

Busy and reactive? Struggling to focus? Craving time for relationships?

If so, perhaps it's time to make space in your world for the things that really matter?

What if you could be productive and rested by living an ordered, rhythmical life? What if habitually unplugging from digital technology was not simply a means of surviving week by week but a strategy to produce your best work and live your best life?

Spacemaker has won six awards including an Axiom Business Book Award in 2023 (USA) and Australian Business Book Award in 2021.

You can purchase the paperback, e-book or audiobook at most online bookstores or scan the QR code below to go directly to my website.

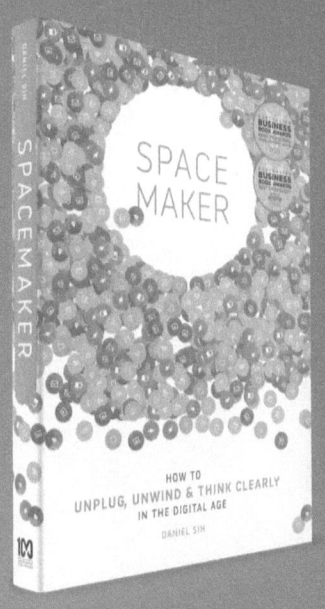

'Read this book.'
— **JACK RIEWOLDT**, AFL PREMIERSHIP VICE-CAPTAIN

'A gem.'
— **ALAN HIRSCH**, AWARD-WINNING AUTHOR

'Life changing.'
— **CATH ANDREW**, HEAD OF HR, STARBUCKS AUSTRALIA

LOOKING FOR PRODUCTIVITY TRAINING?

Is your email inbox out of control? Do you struggle to prioritise work and get the right things done?

If so, we invite you to check out our best-selling productivity training courses, such as Email Ninja, Priority Samurai and List Assassin. These training courses can be delivered in-person in Australia, or online anywhere in the world.

We also have a training course called Making Space to help improve the digital wellbeing of hybrid teams.

To find out more about our productivity training courses, scan the QR code to go directly to Daniel's website.

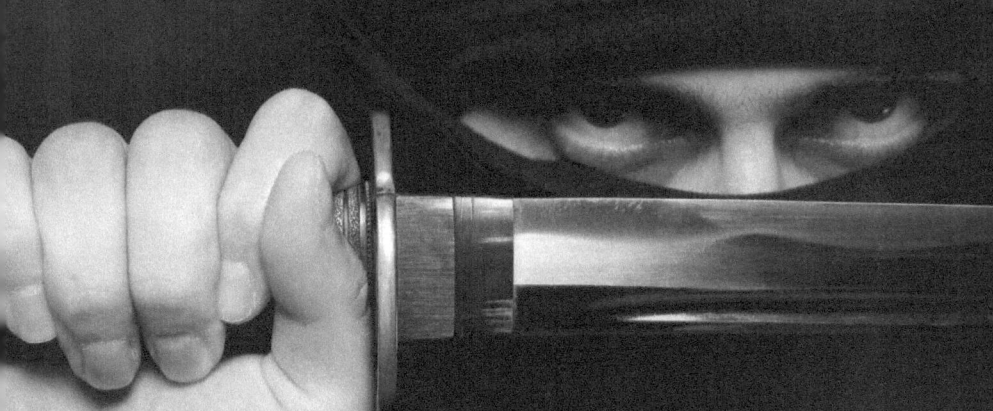

NOTES

1 Raise adults, not children
1. Karen Brooks, *Consuming Innocence: Popular culture and our children* (Queensland: University of Queensland Press, 2008), 260.

2 A healthy brain first
1. Norman Doidge, *The Brain That Changes Itself: Stories of personal triumph from the frontiers of brain science* (Harlow: Penguin Books, 2008).
2. Mariam Arain, Maliha Haque, Lina Johal, Puja Mathur, Wynand Nel, Afsha Rais, Ranbir Sandhu and Sushil Sharma, 'Maturation of the Adolescent Brain', *Neuropsychiatric Disease and Treatment*, 9, 2013, 449–461.
3. Daniel J. Siegel and Tina P. Bryson, *The Whole-Brain Child: 12 revolutionary strategies to nurture your child's developing mind* (New York: Delacorte Press, 2011), 54–59.
4. Ibid, 17–18.
5. Victoria L. Dunckley, *Reset Your Child's Brain: A four-week plan to end meltdowns, raise grades, and boost social skills by reversing the effects of electronic screen-time* (California: New World Library, 2015), 10.
6. Ibid, 9.
7. Victoria L. Dunckley, 'Gray Matters: Too Much Screen Time Damages the Brain: Neuroimaging research shows excessive screen time damages the brain', *Psychology Today*, 27 February 2014, https://www.psychologytoday.com/us/blog/mental-wealth/201402/gray-matters-too-much-screen-time-damages-the-brain.
8. Ibid.
9. Nicholas Kardaras, *Glow Kids: How screen addiction is hijacking our kids – and how to break the trance* (New York: St. Martin's Press, 2016), 4.
10. Ibid, 20.
11. Victoria L. Dunckley, 'Gray Matters: Too Much Screen Time Damages the Brain: Neuroimaging research shows excessive screen time damages the brain', *Psychology Today*, 27 February 2014,

https://www.psychologytoday.com/us/blog/mental-wealth/201402/gray-matters-too-much-screen-time-damages-the-brain.

12 Ibid, 60–63.
13 David Murrow, *Drowning in Screen Time: A lifeline for adults, parents, teachers, and ministers who want to reclaim their real lives* (Washington: Salem Books, 2020), 83.
14 Brien Holden, Timothy Friche, David Wilson, Monica Jong, Kovin Naidoo, Padmaja Sankaridurg, Tien Wong, Thomas Naduvilath and Serge Resnikoff, 'Global Prevalence of Myopia and High Myopia and Temporal Trends from 2000 through 2050', *Journal of American Academy of Opthalmology*, 123 (5), 2016; 1036-1042.
15 Debbie Jones and Kate Gifford, 'How Remote Learning Is Damaging Children's Eyesight', *The Educator Australia*, 12 August 2021, https://www.theeducatoronline.com/k12/news/how-remote-learning-is-damaging-childrens-eyesight/278313.
16 Jiaxing Wang, Ying Li, David Musch, Nan Wei, Xiaoli Qi, Gang Ding, Xue Li, Jing Li, Linlin Song, Ying Zhang, Yuxian Ning, Xiaoyu Zeng, Ning Hua, Shuo Li, Xuehan Qian, 'Progression of Myopia in School-Aged Children After COVID-19 Home Confinement', *JAMA Opthalmology*, 139 (3), 2021; 293-300.
17 The PedsDocTalk podcast, Episode 111, 'The Relationship Between Screen Time and Visual Conditions in Children', https://pedsdoctalk.com/podcast/episode-111-the-relationship-between-screen-time-and-visual-conditions-in-children/
18 Steven Higgins, ZhiMin Xiao and Maria Katsipataki, 'The Impact of Digital Technology on Learning: A Summary for the Education Endowment Foundation. Full Report', *ERIC*, 2012.
19 Zainab Alimoradi, Chung-Ying Lin, Anders Brostrom, Pia H. Bülow, Zahra Bajalan, Mark Griffiths, Maurice Ohayon, Amir Pakpour, 'Internet addiction and sleep problems: A systematic review and meta-analysis', *Sleep Medicine Reviews*, 47, 2019; 51–61.
20 Nicholas Kardaras, *Glow Kids: How screen addiction is hijacking our kids – and how to break the trance* (New York: St. Martin's Press, 2016).
21 Ibid, 34.

3 Life-giving limits

1. Anagha Joshi and Trina Hinkley, 'Too Much Time on Screens? Screen time effects and guidelines for children and young people', Australian Institute of Family Studies, Australian Government, August 2021, https://aifs.gov.au/resources/short-articles/too-much-time-screens-screen-time-effects-and-guidelines-children-and
2. An exception is supervised video chat to communicate with family or friends online. Stephanie Papas, 30 June 2022, 'What do we Really Know About Kids and Screens? Research by psychologists and others is giving us a better understanding of the risks and potential benefits of children's and teens' us of digital devices'. American Psychological Association) https://www.apa.org/monitor/2020/04/cover-kids-screens
3. Yusuke Kondo, Tsuyoshi Tanabe, Mikiko Kobayashi-Miura, Hiroki Amano, Natsu Yamaguchi, Masanori Kamura and Yasuyuki Fujita, 'Association Between Feeling Upon Awakening and Use of Information Technology Devices in Japanese Children', *Journal of Epidemiology*, 22 (1), 2012;22,12–20.
4. Greg McKeown, *Essentialism: The disciplined pursuit of less* (United Kingdom: Random House, 2014), 198.
5. Stephen R. Covey, *First Things First* (New York: Free Press, 2003), 103. The late Stephen Covey famously wrote, 'It's easy to say "no!" when there's a deeper "yes!" burning inside.'

Part II: The STARTER Framework

1. Douglas Adams, *The Hitchhiker's Guide to the Galaxy* (New York: Harmony Books, 1980), chapter 22.

4 Start with self

1. This quote is attributed to Ralph Waldo Emerson, as adapted from an essay titled 'Social Aims' published in 1875 – https://quoteinvestigator.com/2011/01/27/what-you-do-speaks.
2. Jaemin Frazer, *Unhindered: The Seven Essential Practices For Overcoming Insecurity* (Australia: Self-published, 2020), 63.

3   Brené Brown, *Daring Greatly: How the courage to be vulnerable transforms the way we live, love, parent, and lead* (New York: Gothan Books, 2012), chapter 7.

5 Take it slowly

1   Finder's Parenting Report: A Report on Family Trends and Finances, October 2021, https://www.finder.com.au/finders-parenting-report-2021.
2   Ibid.
3   '9 in 10 Aussie Teens Now Have a Mobile (and most are already on to their second or subsequent handset)', Roy Morgan, 22 August 2016, http://www.roymorgan.com/findings/6929-australian-teenagers-and-their-mobile-phones-june-2016-201608220922
4   Ian Johnston, 'Apple Guru Kept His Kids Away From iPads', *NZ Herald*, 13 September 2014, https://www.nzherald.co.nz/world/apple-guru-kept-his-kids-away-from-ipads/BBQIHWTCUPLSBXCFOFK6MUQ4UA/?c_id=2&objectid=11323723.
5   Canela López, '7 Tech Executives Who Raise Their Kids Tech-Free or Seriously Limit Their Screen Time', *Business Insider*, 28 September 2019, https://www.businessinsider.in/slideshows/miscellaneous/7-tech-executives-who-raise-their-kids-tech-free-or-seriously-limit-their-screen-time/slidelist/71343150.cms
6   Ellie Silverman, 'Facebook's First President, on Facebook: "God only knows what it's doing to our children's brains"', *The Washington Post*, 9 November 2017, https://www.washingtonpost.com/news/the-switch/wp/2017/11/09/facebooks-first-president-on-facebook-god-only-knows-what-its-doing-to-our-childrens-brains.
7   South Australia Police, 'Unsolved Cases: Richard Kelvin', Crime Stoppers, https://crimestopperssa.com.au/case/richard-kelvin/
8   Samantha Bricknell, 'Trends & Issues in Crime and Criminal Justice', Australian Institute of Criminology, Australian Government, June 2008, No. 359, https://www.aic.gov.au/sites/default/files/2020-05/tandi359.pdf.

It is worth noting that interpreting crime data is complex. In Australia, homicide has reduced since the 1990s, while rates of aggravated sexual assault have increased, partly influenced by greater reporting to police. It is accurate to suggest that the public perception of violence in our society does not match the data.

9 'Suicide & Self-Harm Monitoring', *Australian Institute of Health and Welfare*, Australian Government, https://www.aihw.gov.au/suicide-self-harm-monitoring/data/populations-age-groups/suicide-among-young-people, retrieved August 2022.

10 Jean Twenge, *iGen: Why today's super-connected kids are growing up less rebellious, more tolerant, less happy – and completely unprepared for adulthood* (New York, Simon & Schuster, 2017), 3.

11 Headspace (2020), 'Insights: Experiences of Cyberbullying Over Time Headspace National Youth Mental Health Survey 2020', https://headspace.org.au/assets/Insights-experiences-of-cyberbullying-over-time-National-Youth-Mental-Health-Survey-2020.pdf.

12 Antonia Quadara, Alissar El-Murr and Joe Latham (2017), 'The Effects of Pornography on Children and Young People: An evidence scan', Australian Institute of Family Studies, Australian Government, https://aifs.gov.au/sites/default/files/publication-documents/rr_the_effects_of_pornography_on_children_and_young_people_1_0.pdf.

13 The eSafety Commissioner, 'Innappropriate Content: factsheet', https://www.esafety.gov.au/educators/training-for-professionals/professional-learning-program-teachers/inappropriate-content-factsheet

14 Ljubica Gjorgievska (2022), '20+ Cyberbullying Statistics in Australia [2022]', Take A Tumble, https://takeatumble.com.au/insights/lifestyle/cyberbullying-statistics/

15 Ibid.

16 Nicholas Kardaras, *Glow Kids: How screen addiction is hijacking our kids – and how to break the trance* (New York: St. Martin's Press, 2016), 195–222.

17 Ibid, 220.

18   Julianna Miner, '5 Things I Wish I Knew Before I Gave My Kid Her First Phone', *Mommy Shorts*, 29 July 2019. https://www.mommyshorts.com/2019/07/5-things-i-learned-when-my-kid-got-her-first-phone.html.

6   Age-appropriate setup

1   Jordan Foster, 'Should I Get My Child A Smartphone?', 9 April 2018, YouTube. https://www.youtube.com/watch?v=1lt-qHXdD0s.
2   Nathan W. Mecham, Melissa F. Lewis-Western & David A. Wood, 'The Effects of Pornography on Unethical Behaviour in Business', *Journal of Business Ethics*, 168, 2021; 37–54.
3   Diana Warren and Neha Swami (November 2019), 'The Longitudinal Study of Australian Children – Chapter 5, Teenagers and Sex', Growing Up In Australia, https://growingupinaustralia.gov.au/research-findings/annual-statistical-reports-2018/teenagers-and-sex.
4   Melinda Tankard Reist and Abigail Bray, *Big Porn Inc: Exposing the harms of the global pornography industry* (North Geelong: Spinifex Print, 2011), 29–31.
5   Robert Muratore, Jamin Winans and Kiowa K. Winans (Directors). 26 August 2020. *Childhood 2.0* (Film). Double Edge Films. This quote is from an interview with Chris McKenna, founder of Protect Young Eyes.
6   Jonathan Haidt, 'The Dangerous Experiment on Teen Girls', *The Atlantic*, 21 November 2021, https://www.theatlantic.com/ideas/archive/2021/11/facebooks-dangerous-experiment-teen-girls/620767/
7   Shane Parrish (Host). 2 July 2019. 'Jonathan Haidt: When Good Intentions Go Bad' (No. 61) (Podcast episode). In The Knowledge Project Podcast. https://fs.blog/knowledge-project-podcast/jonathan-haidt/

7   Regular talk

1   Thank you to my friend Michael Frost, who gave me this idea many years ago.

8 Tech-healthy rhythms

1. James Clear, '3-2-1: Paying attention, staying hopeful in bad times, and ten year plans' [blog post], 21 July 2022, https://jamesclear.com/3-2-1/july-21-2022.
2. Steve Simpson, *Unwritten Ground Rules: Cracking the Corporate Culture Code* (Queensland: Narnia House Publishing, 2001), 35.
3. Andy Crouch, *The Tech-Wise Family: Everyday steps for putting technology in its proper place* (Michigan: Baker Books, 2017), 41.
4. Katherine Sellgren, 'Teenagers Checking Mobile Phones In Night', *BBC News*, 6 October 2015, https://www.bbc.com/news/education-37562259.
5. Ibid.
6. Leah Campbell, 'Is Your Teen Getting Enough Sleep? 73% Don't. Here's Why', *Healthline*, 8 October 2019, https://www.healthline.com/health-news/73-of-high-school-students-dont-get-enough-sleep#The-consequences-of-sleep-deprivation-
7. Australian Institute of Health and Welfare, 'Sleep Problems as a Risk Factor for Chronic Conditions', Cat. no. PHE 296, Canberra: AIHW, November 2021, https://www.aihw.gov.au/getmedia/7e520067-05f1-4160-a38f-520bac8fc96a/aihw-phe-296.pdf.aspx.
8. Charles Duhigg, *The Power of Habit: Why we do what we do and how to change* (London: Random House, 2012), 109.
9. Andy Crouch, *The Tech-Wise Family: Everyday steps for putting technology in its proper place* (Michigan: Baker Books, 2017), 155.

9 Encourage adventures

1. Catherine Heuzenroeder, 'Monash Playground Engineer Grant Telfer Remembered For Creating Beloved SA Attraction, *ABC News*, 1 April 2022, https://www.abc.net.au/news/2022-04-01/monash-playground-engineer-grant-telfer-statue-honour/100911254
2. Greg Lukianoff and Jonathan Haidt, *The Coddling of the American Mind: How good intentions and bad ideas are setting up a generation for failure* (New York, Penguin Books, 2018) 163–179.
3. Ibid, 31.

4   Dr Saul McLeod, 'The Zone of Proximal Development and Scaffolding', *Simply Psychology*, 2019. https://www.simplypsychology.org/Zone-of-Proximal-Development.html.

10 Rely on others
1   M. Scott Peck, *The Different Drum: Community Making and Peace* (New York: Simon & Schuster, 1987), 233.
2   Brené Brown, *Daring Greatly: How the courage to be vulnerable transforms the way we live, love, parent, and lead* (New York: Avery, 2012), 30.

Part III: The path forward
1   Chip Heath and Dan Heath, *Switch: How to change things when change is hard* (London: Random House Business Books, 2010), 124-148.

INDEX

Adulthood 5–6, 12, 19
Advert game 73–74
Antifragile 87–88, 92

Boundaries 65–67, 70, 78, 90
Brain 9–20, 26, 46, 72, 88, 95, 112

Car trips 79, 82, 84
Chainsaw 57–58, 67

Digital contract 59–60, 66–67, 108, 112, 119
Downstairs brain 10–11, 13, 95
Dumb phone 108

Electronic device overuse 12–13

Family meal 81

Grade up 59, 67

Hero 54–55, 70
Hyperarousal 13

Internet addiction 14
Internet filters 59, 61–62, 66–67
Leaning back 14, 23
Leaning forward 14, 23
Lost World, The 90–91

Myopia 17–18

Near work 16–18
Nagging 46, 50–52, 55

Parental controls 59, 63–64, 66–67, 78, 84, 108, 112
Pornography xx, 48, 55, 61, 66–67
Predictable patterns 79, 83, 98

Screen time guidelines 22–25, 63
Screen time limits 25
Silicon Valley 46, 51, 55
Slartibartfast 31
Sleep 13, 19, 21, 23, 51, 53, 73, 77, 79–81, 84, 96, 111
Smartphone 15, 45–46, 48–49, 51– 56, 58–59, 64, 67–68, 108

Social media xx, 16, 35, 51, 63–67, 80
Spacemaker 39, 79, 107, 124–125, 145

Token system 24–25
Tough love 6–7, 51, 91

Unplugging 36–37
Upstairs brain 11–12, 19, 95

Video gaming 9, 16
Vulnerability 39–40, 96, 101

ABOUT THE AUTHOR

Daniel is a husband and father of three children, Naomi, Caleb and Jethro, and lives in Tasmania, Australia. He is a productivity expert, an award-winning author, and TEDx speaker who speaks with parents, teachers and leaders about technology and parenting.

Daniel's first book, *Spacemaker: How to unplug, unwind and think clearly in the digital age*, has won six international awards, including an Axiom Business Book Award (USA) in 2023 and an Australian Business Book Award in 2021.

As a productivity trainer, coach and consultant, Daniel has worked with CEOs, executives, and other senior professionals throughout Australia and beyond, ranging from global corporations and businesses to schools and non-profits. He is the founder of a number of globally accessible productivity courses such as Email Ninja®, List Assassin® and Priority Samurai™, with more than 20,000 students online and offline.

As a strategist, Daniel used to enjoy beating his children at board games like Chess, Settlers of Catan and Dominion, but is stuck on a disconcerting losing streak.

To learn more about Daniel and his work, please visit www.spacemakers.au and www.raisinghumans.au.

www.ingramcontent.com/pod-product-compliance
Lightning Source LLC
Chambersburg PA
CBHW030301100526
44590CB00012B/476